Grade 4 • Unit 3

California Inspire Science

Our Dynamic Earth

FRONT COVER: (t to b)Photodigitaal.nl/Shutterstock, Shutterstock/Zadiraka Evgenii, Carlyn Iverson/McGraw-Hill Education, hsvrs/iStock/Getty Images, Shutterstock/vvoe;
BACK COVER: Photodigitaal.nl/Shutterstock; **SPINE** Photodigitaal.nl/Shutterstock

Mheducation.com/prek-12

STEM McGraw-Hill is committed to providing instructional materials in Science, Technology, Engineering, and Mathematics (STEM) that give all students a solid foundation, one that prepares them for college and careers in the 21st century.

Send all inquiries to:
McGraw-Hill Education
8787 Orion Place
Columbus, OH 43240

ISBN: 978-0-07-683502-7
MHID: 0-07-683502-2

Printed in the United States of America.

4 5 6 7 8 9 10 11 12 LWI 25 24 23 22 21 20

Table of Contents
Unit 3: Our Dynamic Earth

Earth and Its Changing Features

Earthquakes

Earth and Its Changing Features

4-ESS1-1, 4-ESS2-1, 4-ESS2-2, 4-ESS3-2, 3-5-ETS1-2, 3-5-ETS1-3

ENCOUNTER THE PHENOMENON

How were these land features formed?

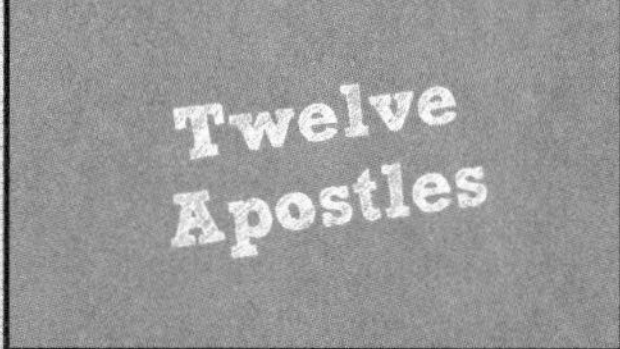

GO ONLINE

Watch the video *Twelve Apostles* to see the phenomenon in action.

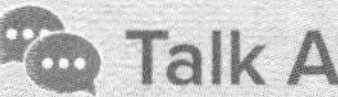

Talk About It

Look at the photo and watch the video of the rock pillars in the water. What do you observe? Talk about your questions with a partner.

Did You Know?

Only 8 of the 12 pillars of the famous Twelve Apostles are still standing today.

STEM Module Project Launch

Engineering Challenge

Don't Get Carried Away

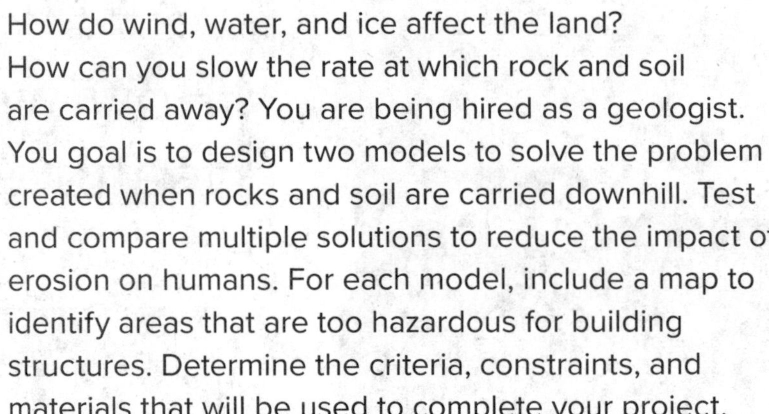

How do wind, water, and ice affect the land? How can you slow the rate at which rock and soil are carried away? You are being hired as a geologist. You goal is to design two models to solve the problem created when rocks and soil are carried downhill. Test and compare multiple solutions to reduce the impact of erosion on humans. For each model, include a map to identify areas that are too hazardous for building structures. Determine the criteria, constraints, and materials that will be used to complete your project.

Lesson 1
Map Earth's Features

Lesson 2
Evidence from Rocks and Fossils

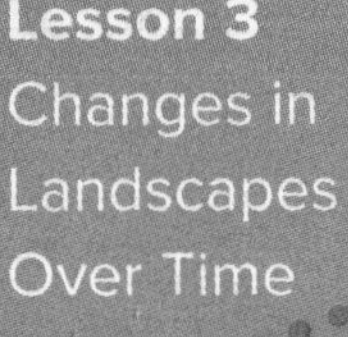

Lesson 3
Changes in Landscapes Over Time

Find multiple solutions to stop soil from moving down a hill.

Geologists study what makes up Earth and the processes that change it. They study and map areas that might be at risk of landslides and other hazards.

MAYA
Geologist

STEM Module Project

Plan and Complete the Engineering Challenge You will use what you learn to design and compare solutions for soil erosion.

PAGE KEELEY SCIENCE PROBES

LESSON 1 LAUNCH

Land and Water Features

Four friends were talking about land and water features such as mountain ranges, volcanoes, ocean trenches, and formations on the ocean floor. They wondered which features occur in patterns. This is what they said:

Woojin: *I think the features on land are the ones that occur in patterns.*

Noah: *I think the features found in oceans are the ones that occur in patterns.*

Abby: *I think both the land and ocean features occur in patterns.*

Elena: *I think land and ocean features occur anywhere. They don't follow any patterns.*

Whom do you agree with most? ______________________________

Explain why you agree.

____

____

____

You will revisit the Page Keeley Science Probe later in the lesson.

LESSON 1

Map Earth's Features

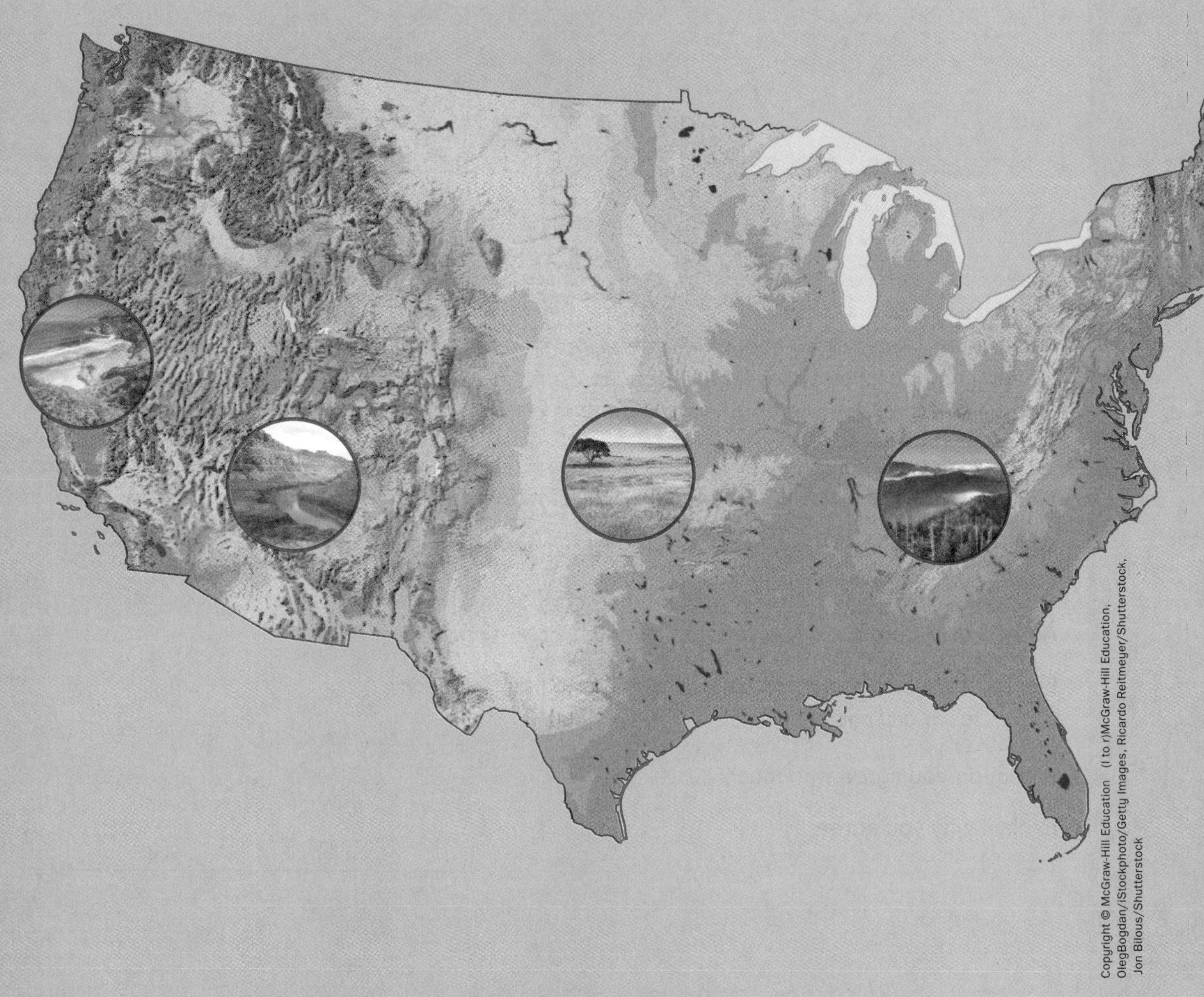

ENCOUNTER
THE PHENOMENON

ESS2.B

What patterns can you find in the locations of Earth's features?

Fields in California

GO ONLINE

Watch the video *Fields in California* to see the phenomenon in action.

Look at the photo and watch the video of the different landscapes across the continental United States. What do you observe? What do you wonder about the map? Write down your observations below.

Did You Know?

Denali, Alaska is the highest elevation in the United States at 6,190 meters (20,310 feet) above sea level. Temperatures can dip as low as -60°C (-75°F).

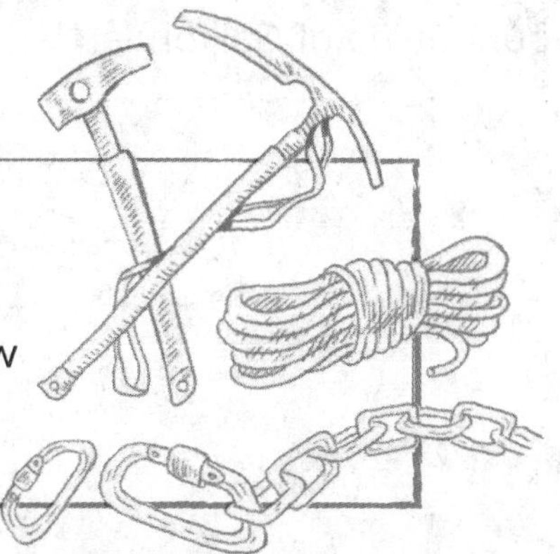

INQUIRY ACTIVITY

Hands On

Map California's Features

Think about the land in your town. Now think about the land in other parts of California. You will design and construct a three-dimensional map of California.

Make a Prediction What properties of landscape features will be important to show in the 3-D model of a California map?

____

____

____

____

____

Carry Out an Investigation

BE CAREFUL Do not eat any of the materials used for this investigation.

1. Glue the outline of California to the sheet of cardboard.
2. Use the spoon and your hands to mix the flour, salt, and water in the bowl. The mixture should make a dough that is easily shaped. If it is still runny after mixing, ask your teacher for more salt and flour.
3. Place the dough on the cardboard and flatten it out to the edges of your outline of California.

Materials

sheet of cardboard (20 x 30 cm)

California outline photocopy

glue

measuring cup

2 cups flour

bowl

1 cup salt

¾ cup water

spoon

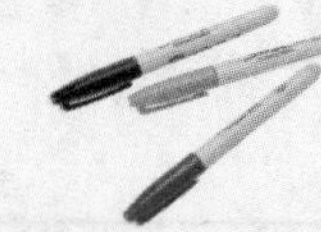
permanent markers

(1)McGraw-Hill Education, (2 5)Joe Polillio/McGraw-Hill Education, (3)Dot Box Inc./McGraw-Hill Education, (4)Michael Scott/McGraw-Hill Education, (6)Jacques Cornell/McGraw-Hill Education, (7 8)Ken Cavanagh/McGraw-Hill Education, (9)Ken Karp/McGraw-Hill Education

4. Use the dough to make landforms in the correct locations. See the map below for reference.

5. Let the dough dry overnight.

GO ONLINE Use the Personal Tutor *Real-World Example: Use Proportions to Solve Problems* to practice how to read a scale on a map.

6. Use teacher-approved websites to label major features on your 3-D map, including cities, mountains, valleys, and bodies of water.

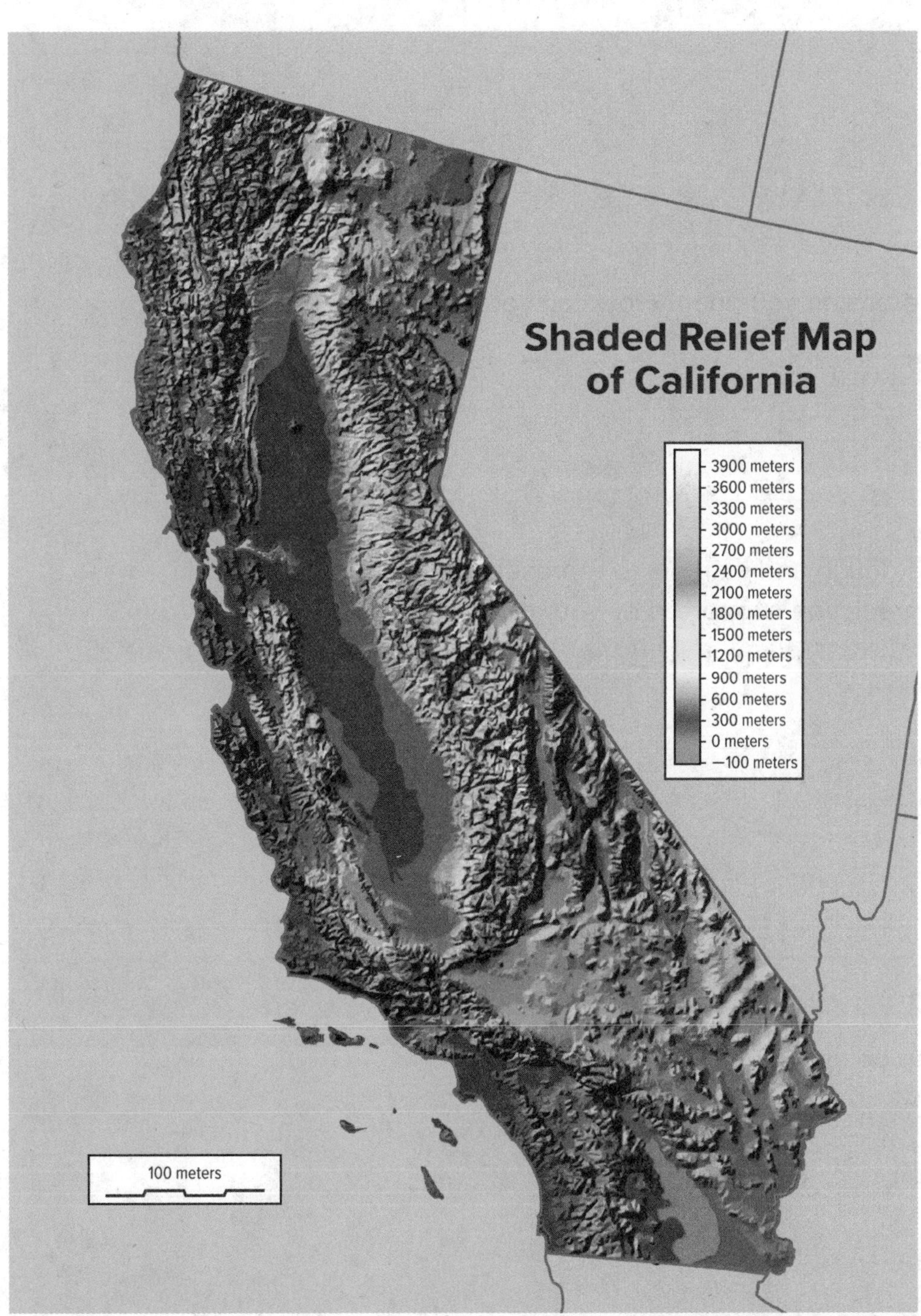

INQUIRY ACTIVITY

Communicate Information

7. Where are the low areas on your map? How can you tell?

8. Where are the high areas on your map? How can you tell?

9. How did you use the dough and markers to represent different features? Was your prediction supported by your observations?

10. How could your map be used?

MAKE YOUR CLAIM

Think of the model you created. What patterns did you notice in the locations of mountains?

Make a claim about patterns of mountain locations.

CLAIM

Mountains are usually located ________________________________

Cite evidence from the activity.

EVIDENCE

In California, mountains are located ____________________________

Add reasoning for your claim, using what you know.

REASONING

You will revisit your claim to add more evidence later in this lesson.

VOCABULARY

Look for these words as you read:

continent

earthquake

landform

latitude

longitude

plate

topographic map

volcano

Landforms

In the Inquiry Activity, *Map California's Features,* you represented different landforms on a three-dimensional map. A **landform** is a physical feature on Earth's surface. Landforms vary greatly in shape and size. They include features such as level plains, rounded hills, and jagged mountains. Each landform has specific characteristics and is formed in a specific way.

Label a Diagram: Earth's Land and Water Features

Use the labels on the image below and descriptions on the next page to learn more about common landforms. Fill in the missing labels using the descriptions.

GO ONLINE Watch the video *Landforms* to see various landforms around the world.

Mountain A landform that rises high above the Earth's surface.

Hill A natural elevation of the Earth's surface, smaller than a mountain.

Valley A valley is the low land between hills or mountains.

Canyon A canyon is a deep valley with high, steep sides.

Plain A plain is a wide, flat area.

Plateau A plateau is flat land that is higher than the land around it.

Desert A desert is an area with very little precipitation.

Beach A beach is the land along the edge of a body of water.

Dune A dune is a mound of sand.

Ocean An ocean is a large body of salt water.

Coast A coast is where a body of water meets land.

River A river is a natural body of moving water.

Lake A lake is a body of water surrounded by land.

Delta A delta is the mass of land that forms at the mouth of a river.

Inlet An inlet is a narrow body of water off a larger body of water.

1. What landforms are near you?

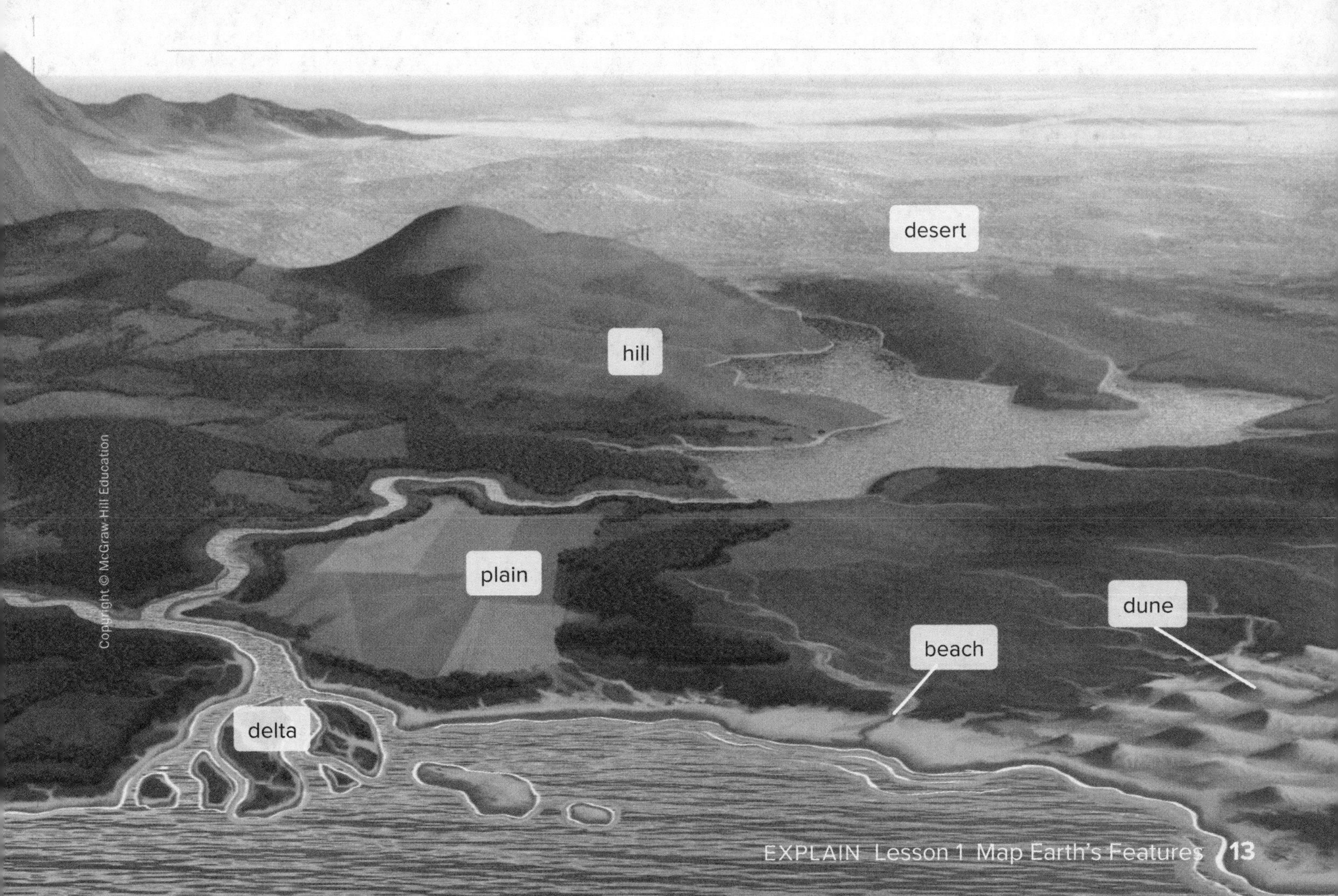

Earth's Ocean Features

Oceans are large bodies of salt water. They make up more than 70 percent of Earth's surface. If you could travel deep below the ocean's surface, you would find features on the ocean floor that look like the mountains, plains, and valleys on Earth's surface.

A **continent** is a large landmass. Along the coast of a continent, the ocean floor is called the *continental shelf*. Here, the ocean floor is covered by shallow water and gradually slopes down. The continental shelf ends at the point where a sharp downward slope begins. This is called the *continental slope*. This land is the steeper part of the continent that slopes down toward the ocean floor. Underwater canyons can form on the continental slope.

At the base of the continental slope is the continental rise. The continental rise connects the continent with the ocean floor.

1. What is the flattest part of the ocean floor?

Ocean Features

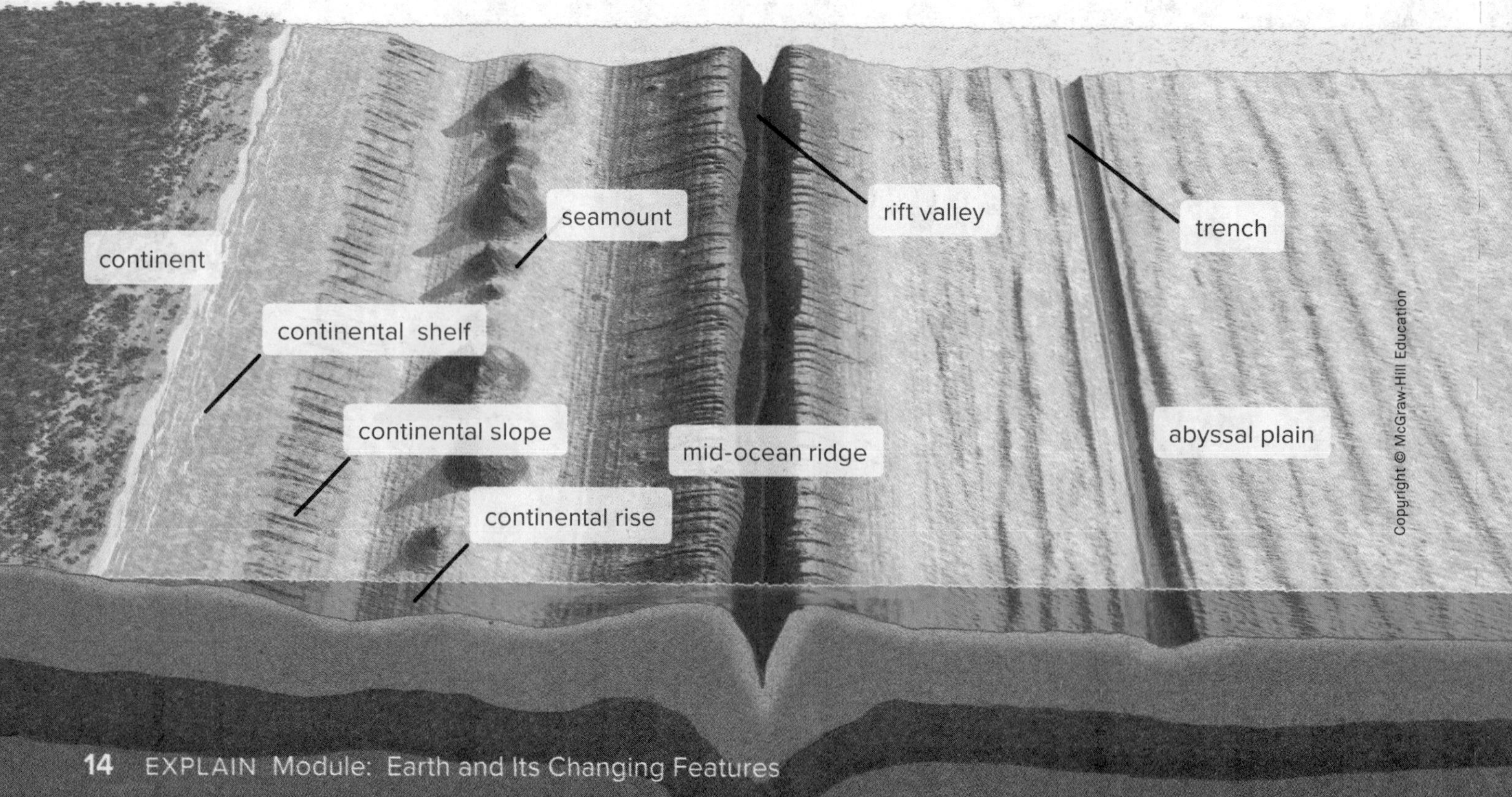

Most of the ocean floor is flat and without features. An abyssal plain is a very flat area of the deep ocean floor. These plains cover about 60 percent of the Earth's surface.

GO ONLINE Watch the video *Ocean Floor* to learn more about these features.

Long mountain ranges stretch through the middle of some oceans. These mountain ranges are called *mid-ocean ridges*. The valley down the center of a mid-ocean ridge is called a *rift valley*.

Other ocean floor features include trenches and seamounts. *Trenches* are the deepest parts of the ocean floor. They are usually long and narrow. A *seamount* is an underwater mountain that rises from the ocean floor but stops before it reaches the surface of the ocean.

Scientists can tell the depth of the ocean floor by sending sounds and waiting for the echo to come back. They also use underwater vehicles to study the ocean floor.

2. Which ocean floor features are underwater mountains?

Pillow lavas along a large fissure on the Galgapagos Rift are located 2,600 meters (1.6 miles) below the ocean surface.

Map Earth's Features

GO ONLINE Explore *Map California* to analyze the patterns and features of California's landscape.

As you have learned, Earth's surface is uneven. Hills rise in one location, and valleys dip in another. The map that you made in the Inquiry Activity, *Map California's Features* was not flat, but most maps of Earth's surface are. How can a flat map show an uneven surface?

There are many different kinds of maps. Physical maps show the features of Earth's land and water. Mountains, deserts, and plains are often shown on physical maps. Some physical maps use shading or lines to represent changes in elevation. *Elevation* is the height of the land above sea level. A map that uses shading to show elevations is called a *relief map*. Relief maps can also reveal patterns in an area.

Read a Map: Nunivak Island, Alaska

Using the key, circle the highest part of Nunivak Island on the relief map below.

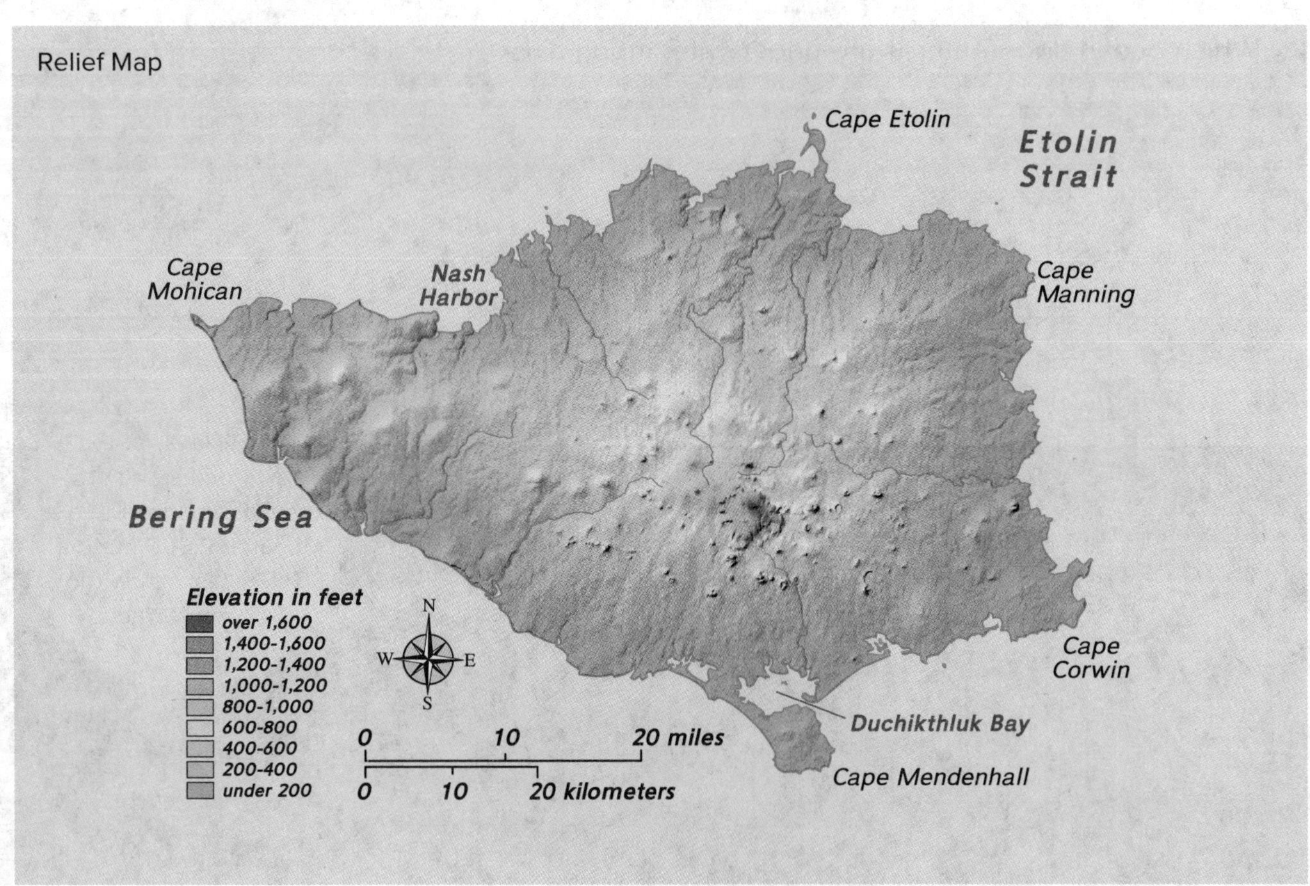

A **topographic map** shows the elevation of an area using lines. Each line is labeled with a number. Contour lines that are close together represent a rapid change in elevation. Contour lines that are far apart represent gradual change in elevation.

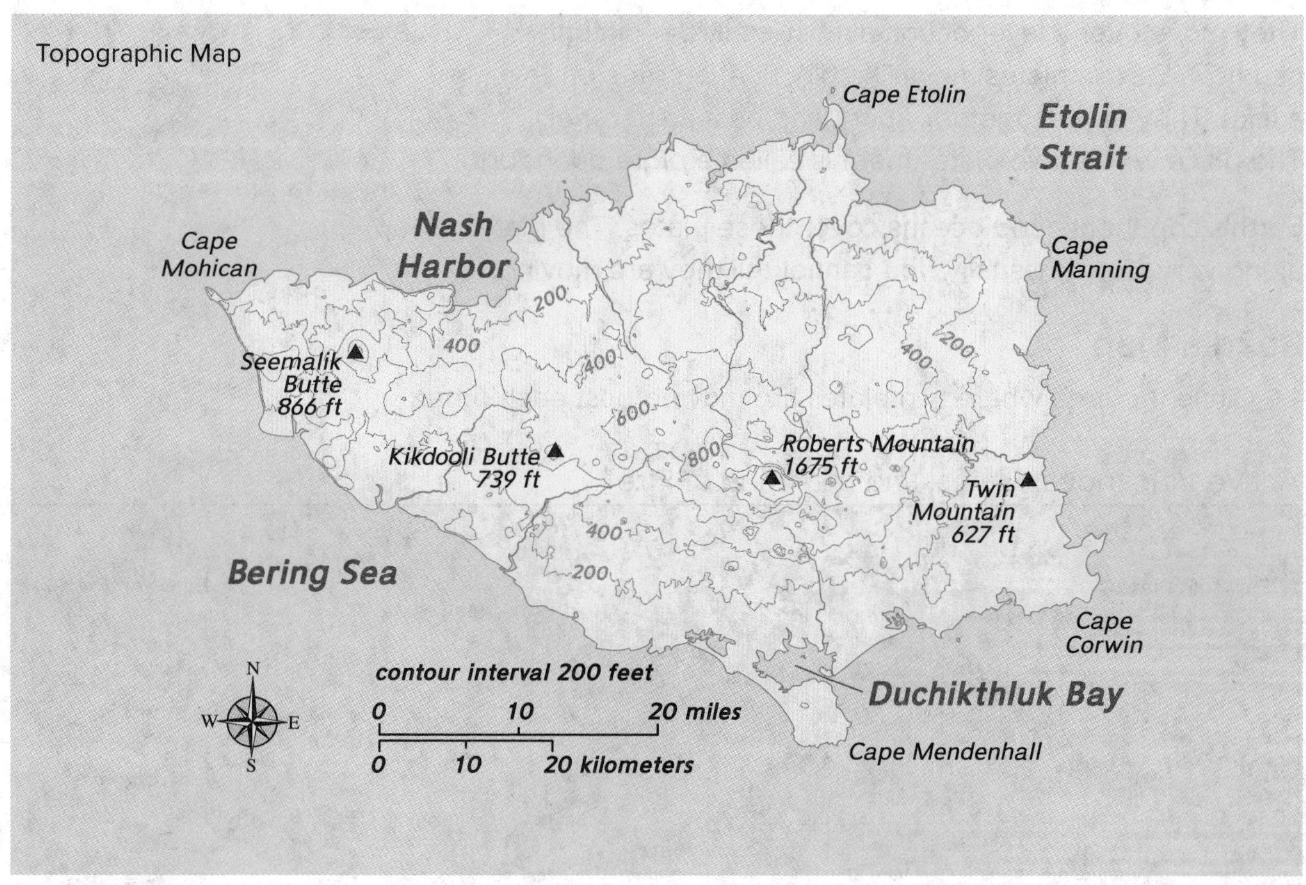

Scientists can use maps to identify patterns in the locations of landforms and other features. The locations of certain features can be described using a coordinate system such as latitude and longitude. **Latitude** is used to describe how far north or south a place is from the equator. **Longitude** is used to describe how far east or west a place is from the Prime Meridian. Latitude and longitude lines form a grid across the globe.

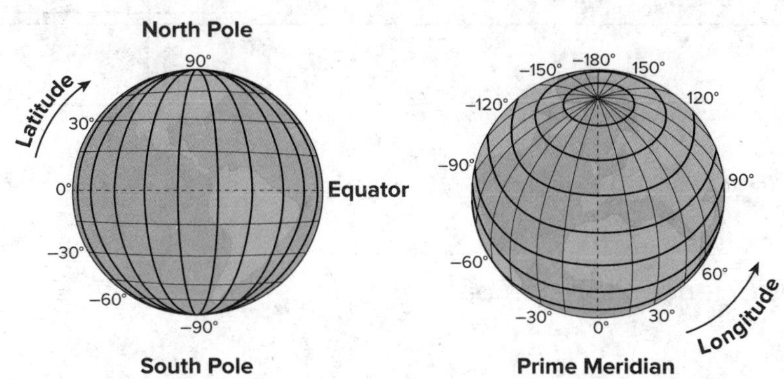

Our Puzzle Planet

Earth has an outer layer of solid rock called the crust. The crust is broken into very large pieces called **plates**. The plates fit together like the pieces of a jigsaw puzzle. They move over a layer of hot, almost-melted rock that can flow. Earth's plates move like big, floating rafts on a lake. They move together, apart, and past each other. The place where two plates meet is called a *plate boundary.*

Earth's continents and oceans cover these plates. The plates creep along very slowly. Usually, you cannot tell they are moving.

Read a Map

1. Circle the area where two plates are moving past each other.

Active Volcanoes, Plates, and the "Ring of Fire"

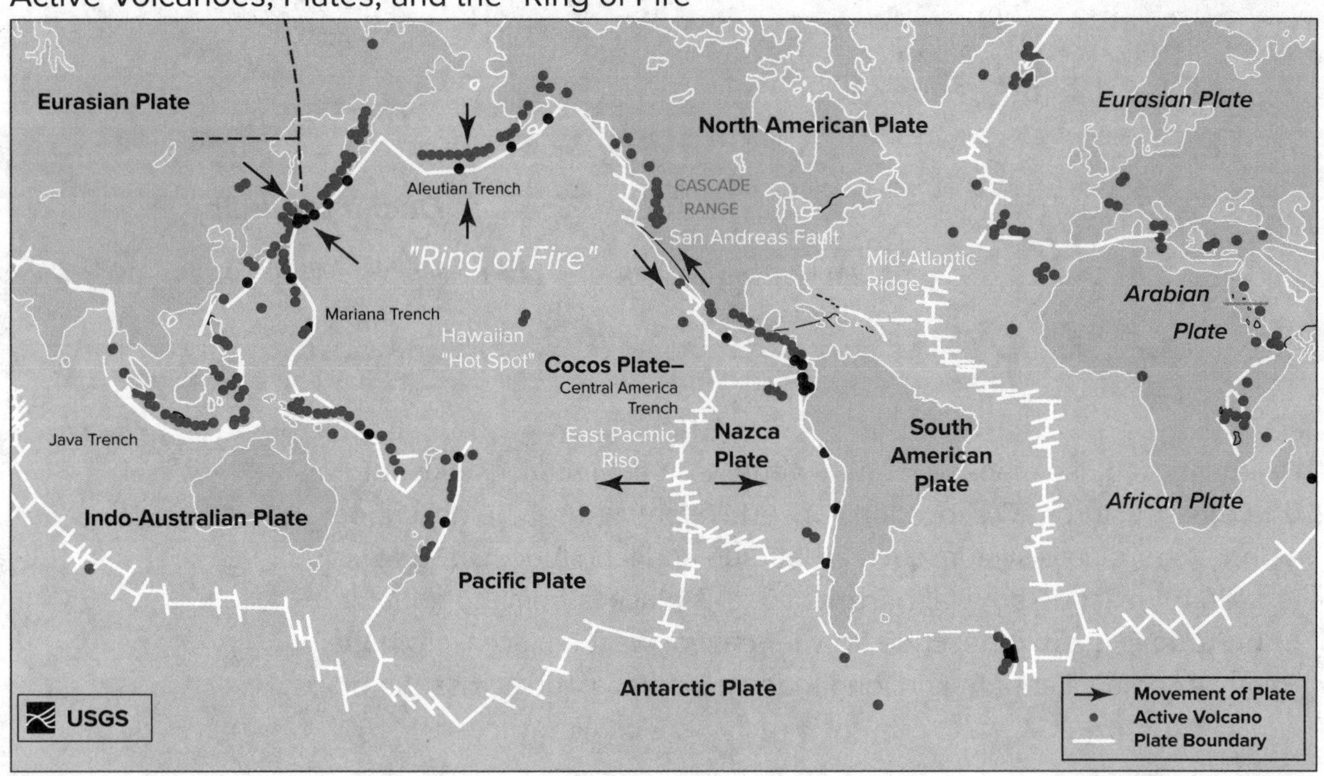

COLLECT EVIDENCE

Use the map to add evidence to your claim on page 11.

REVISIT Revisit the Page Keeley Science Probe on page 5.

Tension, or forces that pull things apart, moves Earth's plates. Plates can also be moved by pushing forces. Mountains form when plates push together or past each other along plate boundaries. Many earthquakes and volcanoes also happen at plate boundaries.

A **volcano** is an opening on Earth's surface where melted rock or gases are forced out. Volcanoes can form on land or on the ocean floor, but they are located only in certain places on Earth's surface. Most volcanoes form at plate boundaries. For example, a ring of volcanoes called the *Ring of Fire* surrounds the Pacific Ocean. The Ring of Fire follows the boundaries of the plates that meet around the Pacific Ocean.

An **earthquake** is a sudden movement of Earth's crust. Like volcanoes, most earthquakes occur because of moving plates. Also, like volcanoes, earthquakes are most likely to occur near plate boundaries. You will learn more about earthquakes in the next module.

2. Describe the global patterns of volcanoes and earthquakes that are shown on the world map.

Think about the ocean floor features from page 14. Some of these features, like ocean trenches, occur where two plates push together. Mid-ocean ridges occur where to plates spread apart. As the two plates move apart, new crust forms. The mid-ocean ridges are all connected and form the most extensive underwater mountain sytem on Earth.

3. Use the graphic organizer to classify the location of the following features: abyssal plains, earthquakes, mountains, volcanoes.

Near Plate Boundaries	Not Near Plate Boundaries

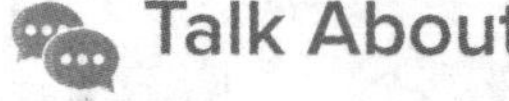

Talk About It

Explain to a classmate where you would most likely find mountain ranges on the ocean floor.

STEM CAREER Connections

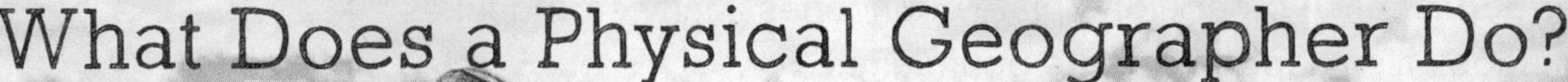

What Does a Physical Geographer Do?

Physical geographers use physical maps to look for patterns in climate data, soil type, or water distribution. They might also look for patterns in the locations of certain types of landforms or natural hazards, such as earthquakes or volcanic eruptions.

Long ago, physical geographers used paper maps to plot data, and make measurements. Today, they use several different technologies to make their work more efficient. Global positioning systems (GPS), remote sensing, and online mapping tools are a few of these technologies. GPS uses satellites to generate accurate location information. Remote sensing uses satellites or aircraft to get information about Earth from a distance.

It's Your Turn

Now you will make your own map. Like a physical geographer, you will use it to describe the location and shape of a model landform.

INQUIRY ACTIVITY

Hands On

Map the Ocean Floor

Have you ever been on a boat and wondered how deep the water was? We cannot see most parts of the ocean floor, but we know that scientists use different tools to measure underwater landforms and create topographic maps.

State the Claim How can depth measurements be used to make a map of something that cannot be seen?

Materials

- shoebox
- sharpened pencil
- drinking straw
- ruler

Carry Out an Investigation

1. Use the ruler to make horizontal lines across the box every 2 centimeters and vertical lines every 2 centimeters.
2. Use a sharpened pencil to poke a hole through the box at every intersection of the horizontal and vertical lines. The hole should be large enough for the straw to fit through.
3. Draw a grid on the next page to match the grid on the shoebox.
4. Label each of the vertical lines on both grids with letters. Label each of the horizontal lines on both grids with numbers.
5. **Record Data** Gently drop the measuring straw in point A1 on your grid. Record the depth measurement of the straw, to the nearest centimeter, on your grid.
6. Move to point A2 on your grid, and repeat step 5. Continue this process until you have measured the depth at each hole.

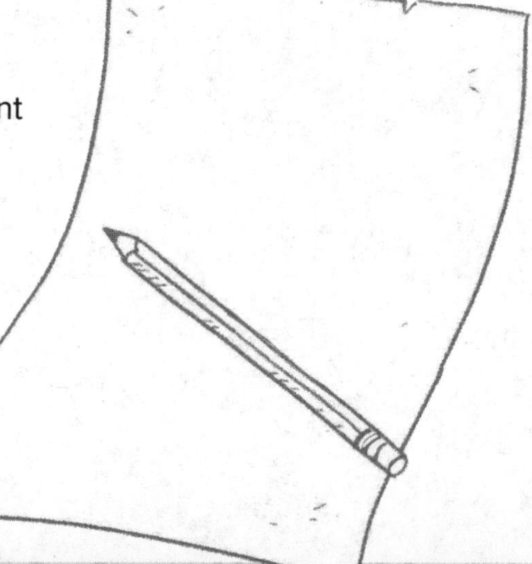

INQUIRY ACTIVITY

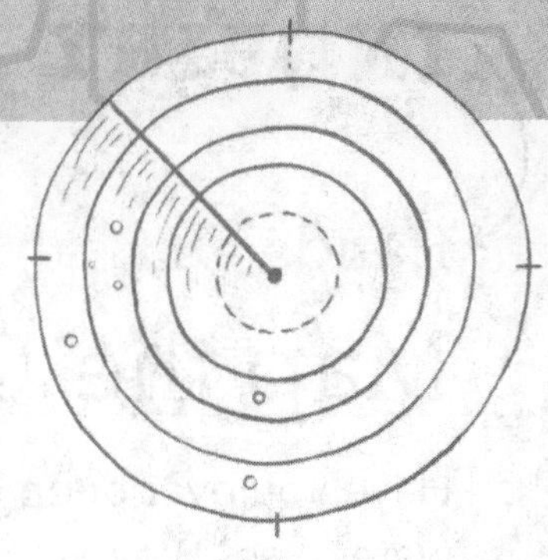

7. Use your probe measurements to figure out the height of the clay in each hole. Record the height on the grid below.

8. Connect equal height measurements using contour lines to create a topographic map of the landform.

9. Remove the lid and compare your drawing to the landform in the box.

Communicate Information

10. How did you use your depth measurements to calculate the height of the landform?

11. How did you use depth measurements to make a map? Use evidence to support your claim.

SEP DCI CCC

Analyze and interpret data to describe how the shape of the clay landform compares to your **model**. What **patterns** do you see?

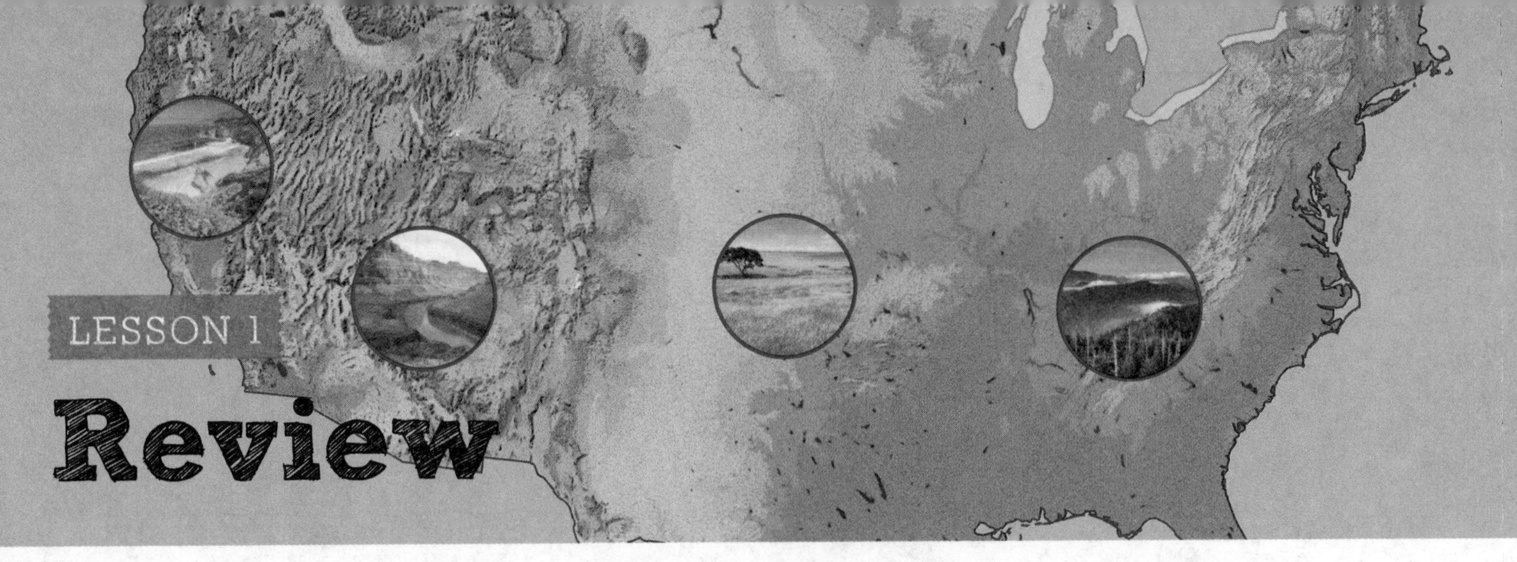

Review

EXPLAIN THE PHENOMENON

What patterns can you find in the locations of Earth's features?

Summarize It

Describe the patterns in the locations of Earth's features, such as mountains, ocean floor structures, volcanoes, and earthquakes.

REVISIT

Revisit the Page Keeley Science Probe on page 5. Has your thinking changed? If so, explain how it has changed.

Three-Dimensional Thinking

1. Which feature is most likely to occur near the edge of a continent?

   A. plain

   B. mountain

   C. lake

   D. abyssal plain

2. Where would you most likely find volcanoes?

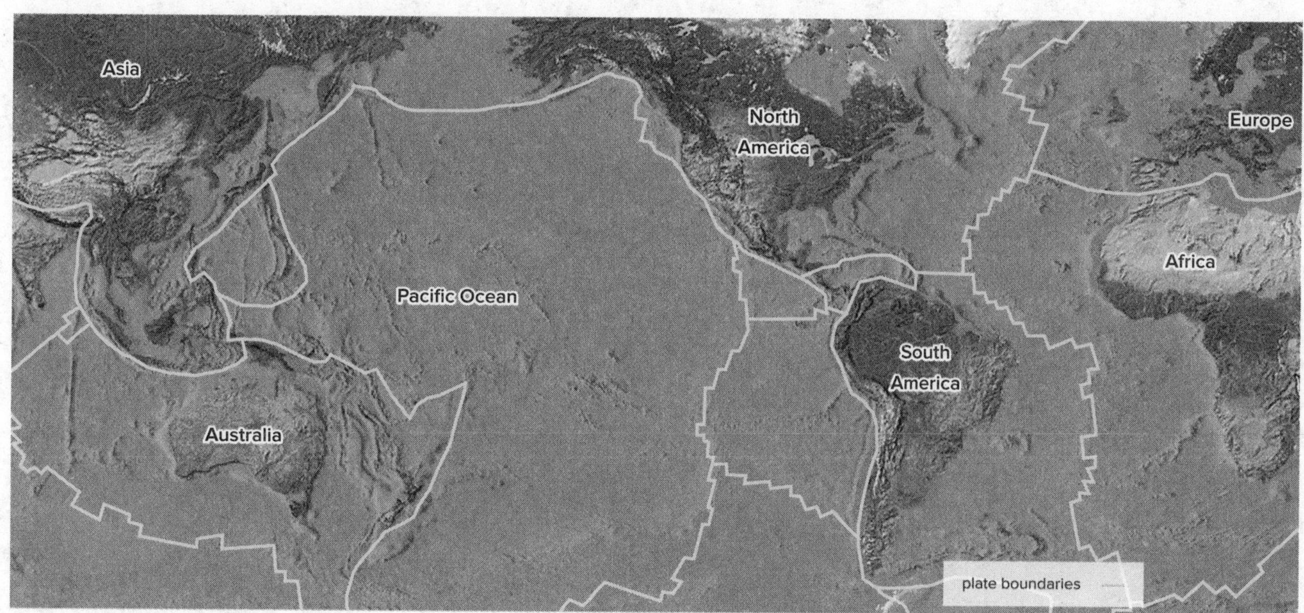

3. Observe the photo above. What ocean features can be mostly found away from plate boundaries?

   A. trenches

   B. seamounts

   C. mid-ocean ridges

   D. abyssal plains

Extend It

You learned that physical geographers use different types of technology for mapping, including global positioning systems (GPS) and remote sensing. Choose a technology and make a television news report explaining how it is used to find patterns. Outline your news report below.

What questions do you still have about how Earth's features are mapped?

Plan and carry out an investigation or research to find the answer to your question.

KEEP PLANNING

STEM Module Project
Engineering Challenge

Now that you have learned about Earth's features and how they are mapped, go to your Module Project to explain how the information will affect your model.

PAGE KEELEY SCIENCE PROBES

LESSON 2 LAUNCH

Information from Layers of Rock

Four friends were looking at the layers of rock in a canyon. They each had different ideas about what scientists learn by examining the rock layers. This is what they said:

Anita: *I think scientists examine rock layers to learn about organisms that lived in the past.*

Mason: *I think scientists examine rock layers to learn about how the surface of the Earth changes over time.*

Aaron: *I think scientists examine rock layers to learn about organisms that lived in the past and how the surface of the Earth has changed.*

Owen: *I don't think rock layers help scientists learn about organisms that lived in the past or how the surface of the Earth has changed. They examine rock layers to identify rocks and minerals.*

Whom do you agree with most? ______________________________

Explain why you agree.

____

____

____

You will revisit the Page Keeley Science Probe later in the lesson.

LESSON 2

Evidence from Rocks and Fossils

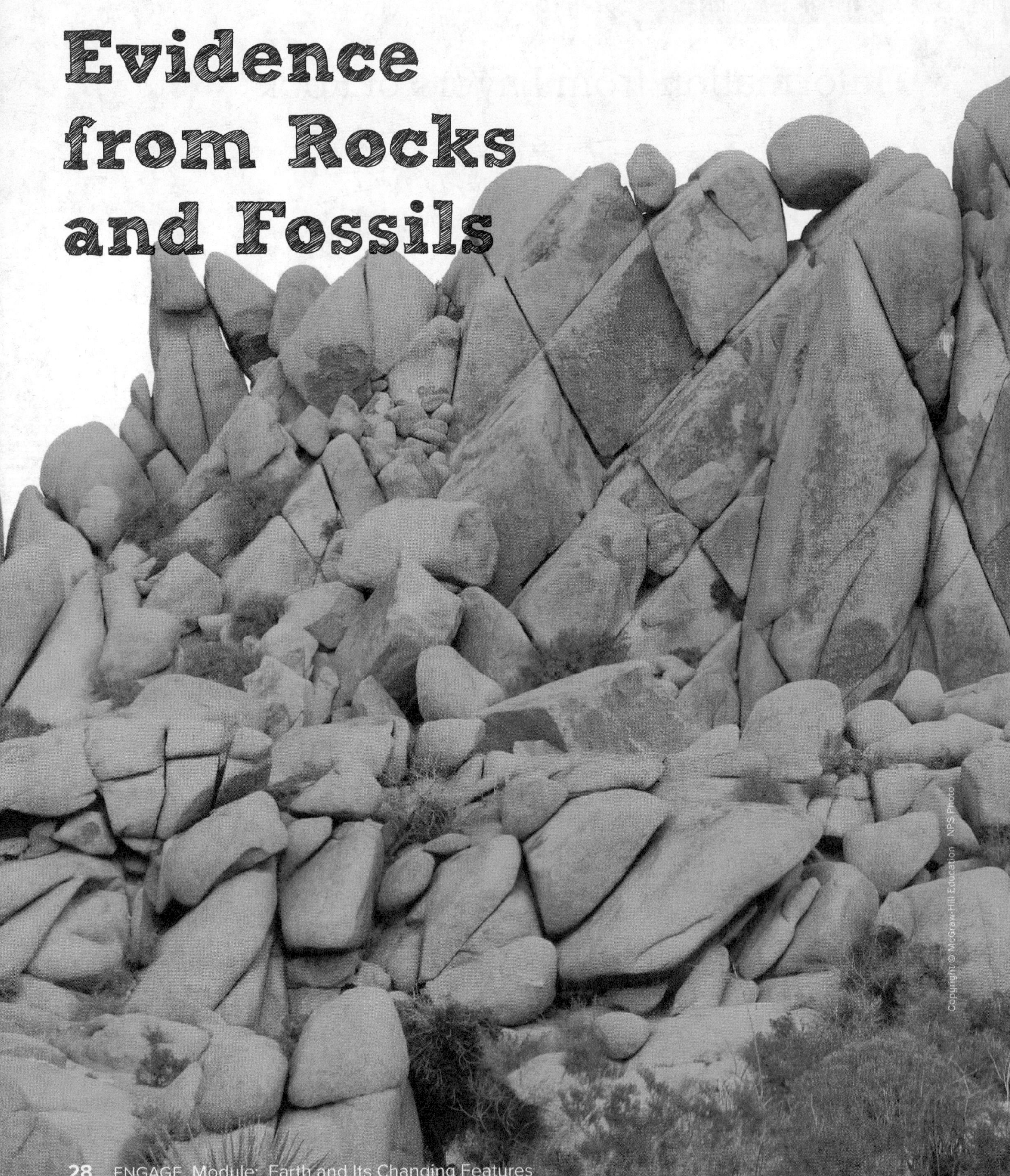

ENCOUNTER
THE PHENOMENON

ESS1.C

What information can we get from rocks?

Watch the video *Rocky Peak* to see the phenomenon in action.

Look at the photo and watch the video of the different rock formations across the state of California. What do you observe? What questions do you have about these rocks? Write down your observations below.

Did You Know?

Many of the rock formations throughout Joshua Tree National Park began forming approximately 100 million years ago.

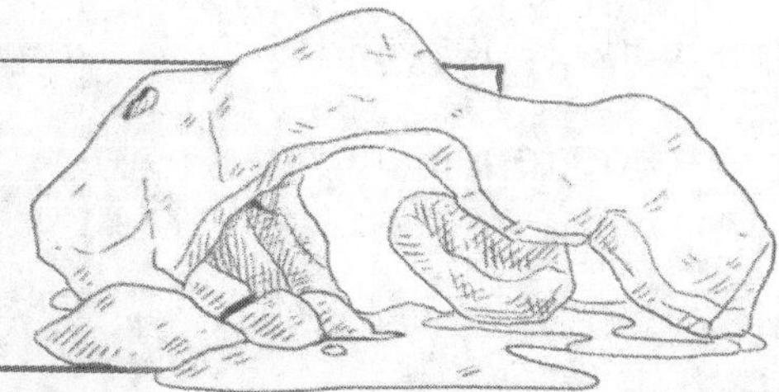

INQUIRY ACTIVITY

Simulation

Fossil Dig

Have you ever stacked newspapers in a pile by placing the latest one on top? After a week, where would you find the oldest news in your stack? Just like your stack of newspapers, rock layers are stacked with the oldest layer found deep in the ground. Suppose you found a fossil. What might that fossil tell you about that layer of rock?

GO ONLINE

Use the simulation *Fossil Dig* to investigate layers of rocks and interpret the fossil evidence found at the dig site.

Make a Prediction What happens to the age of fossils as you dig deeper into rock layers?

Carry Out an Investigation

1. Starting with Area 1, use the shovel tool to dig up each layer of rock. Click on each fossil found and tell where it lived and if it is older than the fossil found in the layer before.
2. Record your observations in the table. Use a separate piece of paper if needed.
3. Dig up Area 2 and repeat step 1.
4. Dig up Area 3 and repeat step 1.
5. Dig up Area 4 and repeat step 1.

Communicate Information

Area	Observations
Area 1	
Area 2	
Area 3	
Area 4	

6. What can you tell about the fossils found near each other in the same layer of rock?

Construct an explanation by using the **pattern** in the fossil dig as evidence to support a claim about the environment over time.

Talk About It

Did your observations match your prediction? Explain your findings to a partner.

What Fossils Tell Us

VOCABULARY

Look for these words as you read:

fossil

sediment

sedimentary rock

Sedimentary rock forms from sediments that are pressed together in layers. **Sediments** are tiny bits of soil or rock that have been broken down and deposited. Wind and water deposit most of the sediments. Over time, layers of sediments are formed with new sediments, which are deposited on top of older layers. Sedimentary rocks are formed by the weight of the top layers or of water covering the sediment pressing the sediment together. It can take millions of years for sediment to become rock.

Fossils, remains or imprints of living things from the past, are preserved in sedimentary rocks. Fossils give scientists information about environments of the past. Ammonites once lived in Earth's oceans. Ammonite fossils are found in rock that is now on dry land. This indicates that the land was once covered by water.

Ammonites lived in water. These fossil ammonites were found on land.

Scientists can also determine the relative age of fossils based on the layer of rock in which they are found. Some fossils also provide clues to a rock layer's relative age. How deep an organism is buried also gives clues as to when the organism lived. Fossils found in layers closest to the surface are usually younger than fossils that are found in deeper layers of rock.

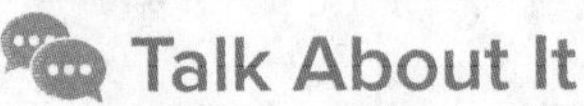

Talk About It

What are the differences and similarities between sediment and sedimentary rock? Discuss with a partner.

GO ONLINE Watch the video *Fossils* to learn more about how they form.

1. How can scientists use evidence from fossils to determine changes in landscape over time? Give an example.

2. **WRITING Connection** Revisit the Inquiry Activity, *Fossil Dig*. Choose one of the areas in which you dug up fossils and write a time sequence story of what was happening at that site in the geologic past. Include at least three characters and dialogue in your story.

GO ONLINE to watch *Fossil Dig* and learn how paleontologists find and recover fossils.

Inspect

Read *Earth Forces* to learn about factors that affect rock layers. Underline in the passage the evidence about the formation of new rock layers.

Find Evidence

Reread the passage. Discuss with a partner. How did the author organize the ideas in the passage?

Reread the passage. How did the author use photos to engage the reader?

Notes

Earth Forces

Earth forces can affect the formation and patterns found in rock layers. Some of these forces include volcano eruptions, earthquakes, and the flow of rivers.

When a volcano erupts, it releases rocks, gases, and hot liquid rock called lava. Lava flows onto the surface, it cools, and hardens into new rock. A new layer of rock forms on top of the old layer each time a volcano erupts, like a stack of pancakes. This happens on continents and under oceans. An island can slowly form when enough underwater rock builds up to reach above the ocean surface. The Island of Hawaii formed this way.

Like volcanoes, earthquakes can change Earth's surface. During an earthquake, the sudden slip of two plates can cause cracks or can cause huge rocks to slide up over another layer. These changes can sometimes look like s-shaped folds in the rock layer.

Revisit the Page Keeley Science Probe on page 27.

Slow movements of Earth's plates can be very powerful too. When plates push together, they push up land. Over millions of years, these forces can form mountains. The Rocky Mountains, in Colorado, formed this way.

Water can interrupt a rock layers by slowly removing rock particles. It slowly carves a gap in the layer, like when you cut and remove a piece of cake. Eventually a canyon forms. It took millions of years for the Colorado River to form the Grand Canyon.

1. Use evidence from each photo to support an explanation about how landscapes change over time.

Make Connections

Talk About It

Explain the cause and effect relationship found in the passage. Discuss with a partner.

Notes

STEM CAREER Connections

What Does a Paleontologist Do?

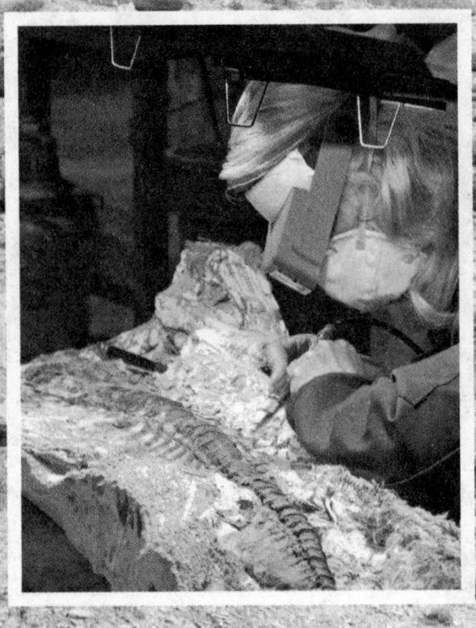

Do you wonder what Earth was like when dinosaurs roamed the planet? Some scientists do too. **Paleontologists** are scientists who study living things, or organisms, that lived long ago. Paleontologists take detailed notes when researching in the field. Most of their work is focused on observing and collecting data from fossilized remains of ancient organisms. These organisms could be plants, animals, or microbes. They could range in size from a microscopic single cell to the fossilized remains of a dinosaur.

Talk About It

Discuss with a partner. How do paleontologists help us learn about Earth's surface?

It's Your Turn

Think like a paleontologist. Complete the activity on the next page to explore the relationship between fossils in rock layers and changes in landscape over time.

INQUIRY ACTIVITY

Hands On

Fossil Model

Materials

multicolored modeling clay

classroom objects

Suppose you had a stack of newspaper on a table. What would happen to the stack if you shook the table? You will create a model that shows fossils and rock layers to explore how scientists learn about how Earth forces might affect rock layers.

Make a Prediction How would your fossil model change if it experienced an earthquake?

Carry Out an Investigation

1. Flatten each color of modeling clay until it is about 1/2 inch thick.
2. Place one or two small objects on top of each layer of modeling clay.
3. Place the layers of modeling clay with the objects on them on top of one another to create a stack of modeling clay of different colors. Press the layers down.
4. Exchange models with a partner. Tell your partner which side of your model is the top layer.
5. Take note of which color is on the bottom.

INQUIRY ACTIVITY

6. **Record Data** Draw and label the model before and after simulating an earthquake.

7. Carefully pull the layers apart and remove the objects. Record which objects you found in which layer in the space below.

Communicate Information

8. What patterns do you notice in the model before and after the earthquake?

9. What causes older fossils to be found on the bottom layer of a fossil dig?

10. How could the flow of a river affect your model? What would happen if the river dried up?

Talk About It

Share your model with a classmate and discuss ideas on how to improve your model so you can show the effect of Earth forces on rock layers.

EXPLAIN THE PHENOMENON

What information can we get from rocks?

Summarize It

Explain how we can learn about the past from rocks and fossils.

REVISIT Revisit the Page Keeley Science Probe on page 27. Has your thinking changed? If so, explain how it has changed.

Three-Dimensional Thinking

1. ________________ form from sediments that are cemented or pressed together.

   A. Sediments

   B. Fossils

   C. Sand

   D. Sedimentary rocks

2. Use an analogy to explain how Earth forces affect the patterns found in rock layers.

3. What evidence can be used to explain the patterns found in rock layers?

Extend It

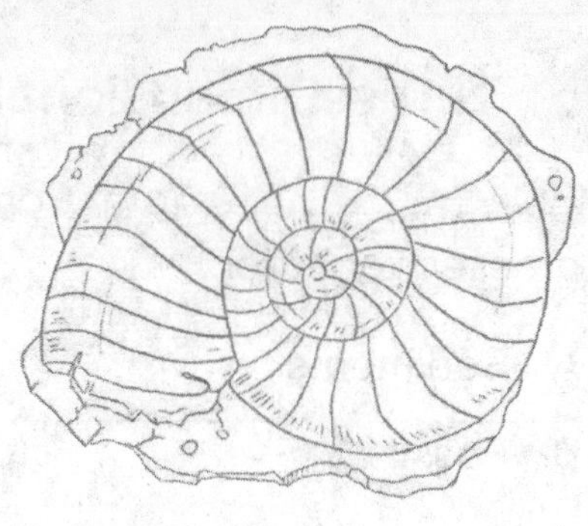

You are a paleontologist. Research the area where you were born. Find out what types of living things lived in your place of birth thousands of years ago.

Write a speech, draw a poster, create a flyer, or use media to communicate your results to your class as a paleontologist.

KEEP PLANNING

STEM Module Project

Engineering Challenge

Now that you have learned about the evidence found in rocks and fossils in rock layers, go to your Module Project to explain how this evidence will affect your plan for your erosion solution design.

LESSON 3 LAUNCH

Changing Landforms

Three friends were talking about processes that change landforms. They each agreed that wind, water, and ice could wear away and change landforms. They disagreed on how long it takes for these processes to change landforms. This is what they said:

Bianca: *I think it takes a long time for these processes to change landforms.*

Rose: *I think it takes a short time for these processes to change landforms.*

Wyatt: *I think these processes sometimes change landforms quickly, but they can also take a long time.*

Whom do you agree with most? ______________________________

Explain why you agree.

____

____

____

____

____

____

You will revisit the Page Keeley Probe later in the lesson.

LESSON 3

Changes in Landscapes Over Time

ENCOUNTER
THE PHENOMENON

ESS2.A, ESS2.E

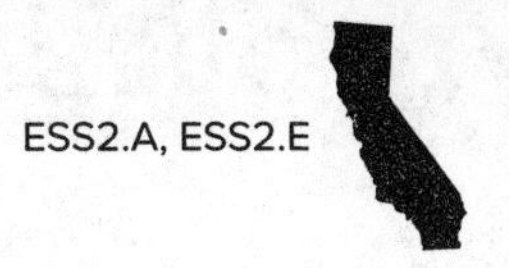

How can moving water change the shape of land over time?

GO ONLINE

Watch the video *San Juan River* to see the phenomenon in action.

Look at the photo and watch the video of the river. What questions do you have about the phenomenon? What do you observe? Record or illustrate your thoughts below.

Did You Know?

The San Juan River flows through a gorge or canyon that measures 300 meters (1,000 feet) deep.

INQUIRY ACTIVITY

Hands On

Shake, Rattle, and Roll

Have you ever seen a "river rock?" They are usually used in landscaping. How would you describe the shape of river rocks? In this investigation, you will model what happens to rocks in fast-moving river water.

Make a Prediction What will happen to rocks if you shake them in a container with water?

Materials

safety goggles

graduated cylinder

3 plastic jars with lids and water

sandstone rocks

stopwatch

hand lens

masking tape

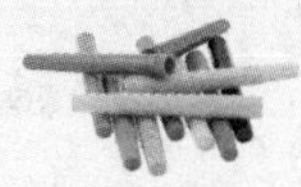
marker

Carry Out an Investigation

BE CAREFUL Wear safety goggles.

1. Label three jars *No Shake, 2-Minute Shake,* and *5-Minute Shake*. Place the same amount of similar-sized rocks in each jar.
2. Using the graduated cylinder, fill each jar with 75 mL of water. Firmly attach a lid on each jar.
3. Let the *No Shake* jar sit. Do not shake it.
4. Shake the *2-Minute Shake* jar hard for two minutes while your partner times the shaking with the stopwatch. Then let the jar sit.
5. Switch roles and use the stopwatch while your partner shakes the *5-Minute Shake* jar for five minutes. Then let the jar sit.
6. Use a hand lens to observe the rocks in each jar. Record your observation in the data table.

	Observations
No Shake	
2-Minute Shake	
5-Minute Shake	

7. What do you think would happen if you shook the jar for an hour?

8. Do the results support your prediction? Explain.

Construct an explanation for what **causes** the rocks in this investigation to change.

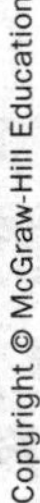

Talk About It

Compare your results with a classmate. How could you improve the design of this investigation?

Weathering

VOCABULARY

Look for these words as you read:

deposition

erosion

vegetation

weathering

Recall the changes that you observed in the Inquiry Activity, *Shake, Rattle, and Roll.* You modeled weathering when you shook the jars. **Weathering** is the slow process that breaks down materials into smaller pieces. This process explains how rocks can change size and shape without changing their chemical properties.

Physical Weathering

Water can seep into cracks in a rock during warm weather. When the water freezes during cold weather, the water expands and makes the crack bigger. This process can also cause potholes and cracks in a road or sidewalk.

Abrasion is the action of rocks and sediments grinding against each other and wearing away surfaces. Abrasion can happen in many ways, such as when rocks and pebbles roll along the bottom of a river. Abrasion also occurs when rocks fall and tumble against one another. The force of the rocks hitting each other knocks off pieces of the rock. Wind causes abrasion. Sand blown by wind against exposed rock wears away the surface of the rock.

Rocks crashing together in a rockslide causes abrasion, a type of physical weathering.

Many animals, like gophers, worms, and ants, can loosen and move soil and break apart rocks as they burrow in the ground. Plant roots can grow inside cracks in a rock and, over time, split the rock into pieces.

GO ONLINE Watch the video *Landscapes Change Over Time* to learn more about these processes.

The actions of living things, such as burrowing animals or growing plant roots, can cause weathering.

What type of force can cause abrasion?

Chemical Weathering

Chemical weathering changes the minerals that make up rocks. Water, living things, and oxygen can cause chemical weathering.

Acids from natural sources, such as volcanoes, can make water more acidic. These acids can speed the breakdown and weathering of rocks.

Iron combines with oxygen in the presence of water to form rust. Rocks that contain iron can rust. Rust makes rock soft and crumbly.

Plant roots give off a weak acid as they grow. Lichens, plant-like organisms that grow on rocks, also produce weak acids. Lichens are important to soil formation in cold climates.

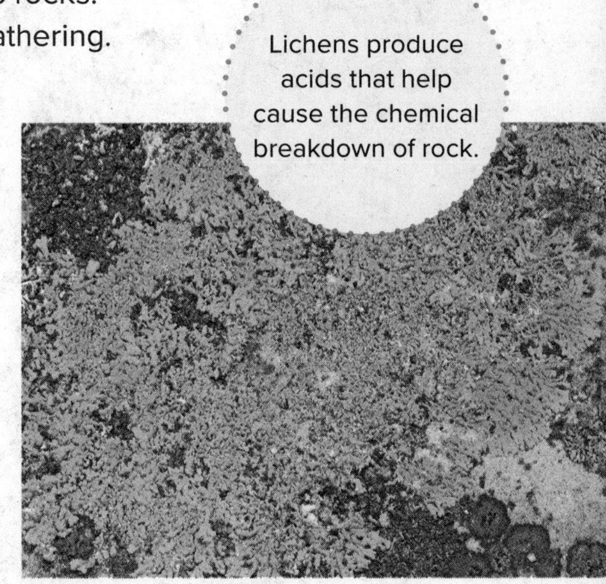

Lichens produce acids that help cause the chemical breakdown of rock.

Erosion and Deposition

Erosion is the movement of weathered material from one place to another. The process of eroded soil and bits of rock being dropped off in another place is **deposition**. Erosion and deposition are two processes that change the shape of land.

Erosion and Deposition by Gravity

Gravity causes material to move. The sudden movement of large amounts of material down a slope can take the form of mudslides, landslides, and rockslides. Strategies such as building away from steep slopes, redirecting surface water away from landslide-prone areas, and planting ground cover to reduce water filtering into the ground can reduce hazardous events such as landslides.

Erosion and Deposition by Running Water

As water runs downhill, it can wash away soil and erode rock. The steeper the land, the faster the water moves. Fast-moving water has more energy. It can wash away larger amounts of heavier sediment. Rivers eventually flow into a larger body of water, such as a lake or an ocean. The sediment carried by the river is deposited on the bottom of the larger body of water. Over time, this sediment builds up into a landform called a delta.

Erosion and Deposition by Wind

Wind can move sand from one place to another. The stronger the wind blows, the larger the particles it can pick up. Deposition occurs when a clump of grass or rock traps the sediment. A sand dune is a deposit of wind-blown sand. Dunes move over time.

Plant roots can help keep a dune from moving.

Erosion and Deposition in Shorelines

> **GO ONLINE** Watch the video *Weathering* to learn more about what shapes the land.

Waves release a lot of energy when they hit the beach. A large wave can break solid rock or throw rocks back against the shore. The rushing water in breaking waves can easily wash into cracks in the rocks, helping to break large boulders. The loose sand picked up by the waves polishes and wears down coastal rocks. Waves can also move sand and rocks and deposit them in other locations, forming beaches. A beach is any area of shoreline made of material deposited by waves. Some beach material is deposited by rivers.

A headland is an area that has water on three sides. Waves curve around a headland and erode the sides. Eventually, the waves change the headland into an arch.

1. Why does fast-moving water have a greater effect on land?

---

2. What are the cause and effect of the changes observed in the photo below?

Erosion and Deposition by Glaciers

Glaciers form where snow collects quickly and melts slowly. As the snow builds higher, the weight of the ice increases, and the glacier starts to move. As it moves, it tears rock from the ground. Glacial till ends up mostly at the end, or terminus, of the glacier.

Erosion and Living Things

Factors such as heavy rainfalls, sparse vegetation, and steep inclines can cause land to erode at a faster rate. Heavy rainfalls can create new flooded habitats for migratory birds and other water dwellers. Fish lay eggs, and crayfish burrow in the fresh mud. Too much rain can also have negative effects on some wildlife. Heavy rains can destroy nests, burrows, and reduce food sources.

Glaciers can erode solid rock! These grooves were formed as a glacier moved across the land.

3. **ENVIRONMENTAL Connection**
How would the rate of erosion of a plain compare to the erosion of the side of a mountain if slope was the only factor to consider?

A Glacier Deposits Land

REVISIT PAGE KEELEY SCIENCE PROBES Revisit the Page Keeley Science Probe on page 43.

FOLDABLES®

Cut out the Notebook Foldables tabs given to you by your teacher. Glue the anchor tab as shown below. Use what you have learned to describe how the terms relate to the image of the sea arch.

GO ONLINE Use the Personal Tutor *Weathering, Erosion, Deposition* to learn about how these processes change the shape of land.

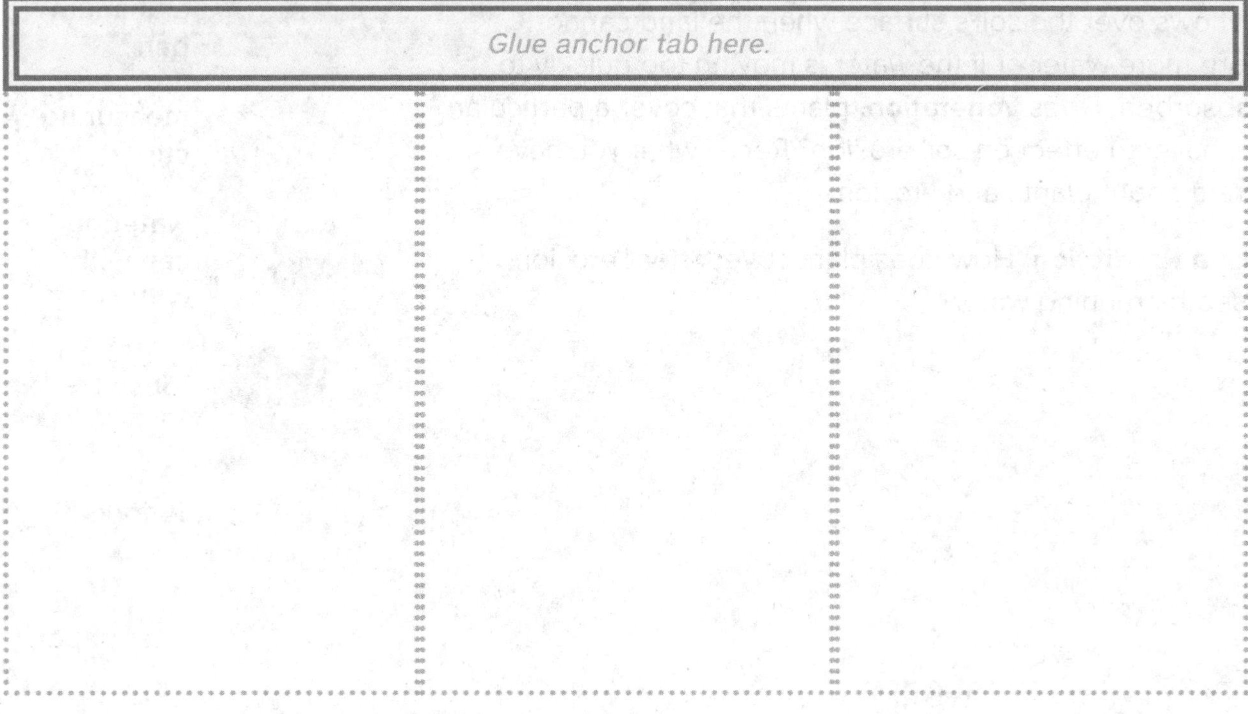

INQUIRY ACTIVITY

Hands On

Effects of Vegetation

Think about where you have seen dirt and mud after a storm. Rain flows over the soil's surface when the land cannot absorb more water or if the water is moving too quickly to be absorbed. Does **vegetation,** plants that cover a particular area, have an effect on soil erosion? Recall what you have learned about plants and erosion.

Make a Prediction How does plant cover affect erosion caused by running water?

____

____

____

____

Materials

2 small aluminum pans

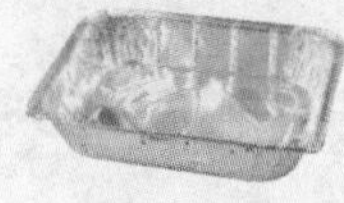
large aluminum pan

measuring cup

watering can with water

topsoil

14 forks

filter paper

funnel

pan balance

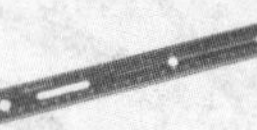
ruler

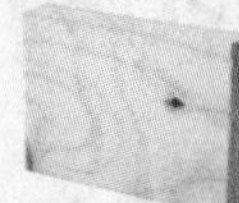
wood block

Carry Out an Investigation

BE CAREFUL Use caution when handling the aluminum pan to avoid injury with the sharp edges.

1. Add soil to a small aluminum pan. The soil should measure 7 centimeters deep. Break up any clumps of soil that are present and pat the soil gently to make it level.
2. Place the wood block under one side of the pan so the pan is propped up 6 centimeters.
3. Position the small aluminum pan inside the larger pan, with the short side opening pointing down.
4. Fill your watering can with 500 mL of water. Tilt the can to simulate a steady, heavy rain over the soil. Let the water drain completely from the small pan.
5. Place a filter paper inside the funnel. Have your partner hold it in place.

GO ONLINE Explore *Factors of Weathering* to match environmental factors to the landforms they shaped.

6. Remove the small pan. Slowly filter the runoff water from the large pan over the sink until the water no longer drips from the funnel.

7. Weigh the amount of soil that was collected. Record this in the data table.

8. Now repeat steps 1–4 using the other small pan. This time you will "plant" forks to represent plants. Be sure to plant the 14 forks with the tines pointing down. The soil should reach the neck of the fork.

Communicate Information

Vegetation	Soil Mass (g)
No plants	
With plants	

9. Compare and contrast your investigation to a real-world situation.

10. Describe the type of erosion to which the soil was exposed in this investigation.

Talk About It

How could you improve this investigation? Tell a partner.

STEM CAREER Connections

What Does a Soil Scientist Do?

John Tatarko is a **soil scientist** at the Wind Erosion Research Unit (WERU) and works on the Wind Erosion Prediction System (WEPS) simulator. He hopes WEPS will help farmers develop better ways to prevent erosion.

When asked "Can a Dust Bowl happen again?" he replied, "If we had weather conditions of the 1930s today for only a few years, wind erosion would not be as severe because of improved farming practices. The extent of drought and winds are up to Mother Nature."

Planning for the rest of the twenty-first century and beyond involves continuing research, practicing good land management, and being prepared.

Stripcropping, cover crops, windbreaks, and terraces are some land management strategies that help reduce soil erosion.

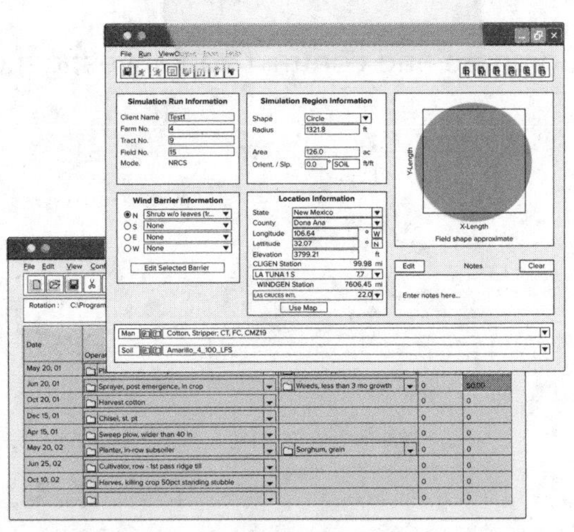

The Wind Erosion Prediction System is a computer simulation program designed to predict soil loss by wind.

It's Your Turn

Think like a soil scientist. You will research and prepare a plan that includes three good land-management strategies. Describe how each contributes to the conservation of Earth's natural resources. List your sources on a separate piece of paper.

GO ONLINE Use the simulation *Effects of Erosion on Landforms* to practice changing factors that affect landscapes.

Talk About It

How can technology help reduce soil erosion? Discuss with a partner.

Strip farming, windbreaks, breakwaters, vegetation, and terracing are some strategies that can help conserve soil.

EXPLAIN THE PHENOMENON

How can moving water change the shape of land over time?

Summarize It

Explain what causes the shape of land to change over time.

Revisit the Page Keeley Science Probe on page 43. Has your thinking changed? If so, explain how it has changed.

Three-Dimensional Thinking

1. Changes in the landscape can be caused by ____________.

   A. physical weathering

   B. chemical weathering

   C. living things

   D. All of the above

2. ____________ is the process that breaks down material.

3. Explain how heavy rainfall can affect the land and living things in an area.

4. What can affect how fast land erodes?

Extend It

You are a soil scientist. Recall what you learned about good land-management strategies. How might you communicate the best strategies that farmers could use to reduce erosion on their land? Write a speech, create a poster, or use media.

What questions do you still have about how landscapes change over time?

Plan and carry out an investigation or research to find the answer to your question.

KEEP PLANNING

STEM Module Project

Engineering Challenge

Now that you have learned about what contributes to the changes in landscape, go to your Module Project to consider this information as you design your soil erosion project.

Don't Get Carried Away

You have been hired as a geologist. Using what you have learned throughout this module, you will work in a small group to design two solutions for soil erosion. You will build and compare the results of two models and select the design that best minimizes the effects of soil erosion. Include an explanation about how your design would affect neighboring property, reduce erosion damage on the land, and protect the environment. On a map, identify hazardous areas where you would not recommend building structures.

Planning after Lesson 1

Apply what you have learned about mapping Earth's features to your project planning.

How can we use maps to describe the shape of the land?

MAYA
Geologist

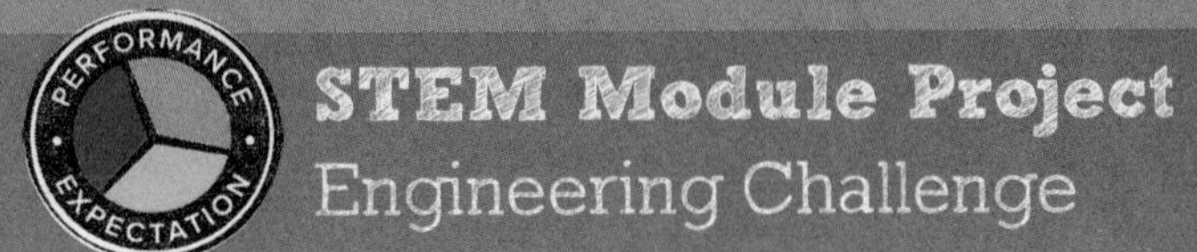

Planning after Lesson 2

Apply what you have learned about evidence from rocks and fossils to your project planning.

How can we use our understanding of Earth forces to explain the changes in a landscape over time?

Planning after Lesson 3

Apply what you have learned about changes in landscape to your project planning.

What factors should be considered when trying to design a solution to erosion?

Research the Problem

Research the factors that help shape the land by reading the *Movers and Shapers* investigator article, going online to teacher approved websites, or by finding books on erosion solutions at your local library.

Sketch Your Model

Draw and label your ideas in the space below. Select two models to build and test.

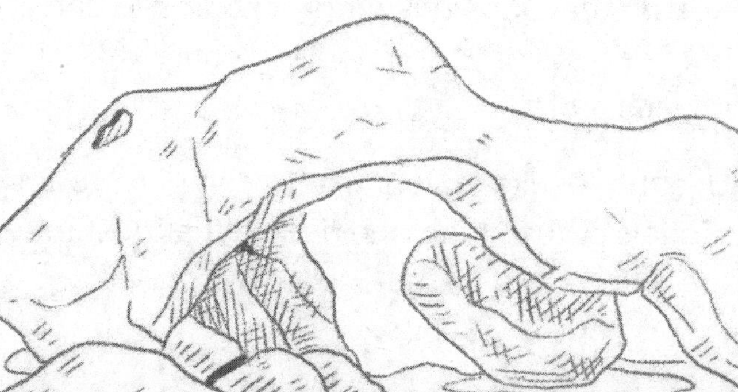

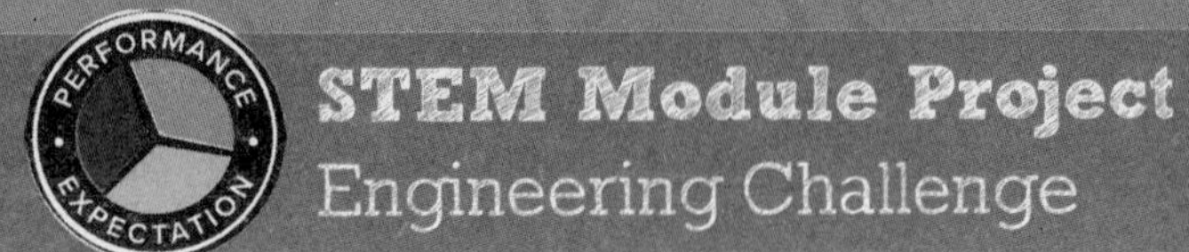

Don't Get Carried Away

Look back at the planning you did after each lesson. Use that information to complete your soil erosion project. As part of the design criteria, your models should be able to hold back soil, and allow water through. The constraints are that your models should be easy to install and should not cause harm to neighboring properties or the environment.

The Engineering Design Process

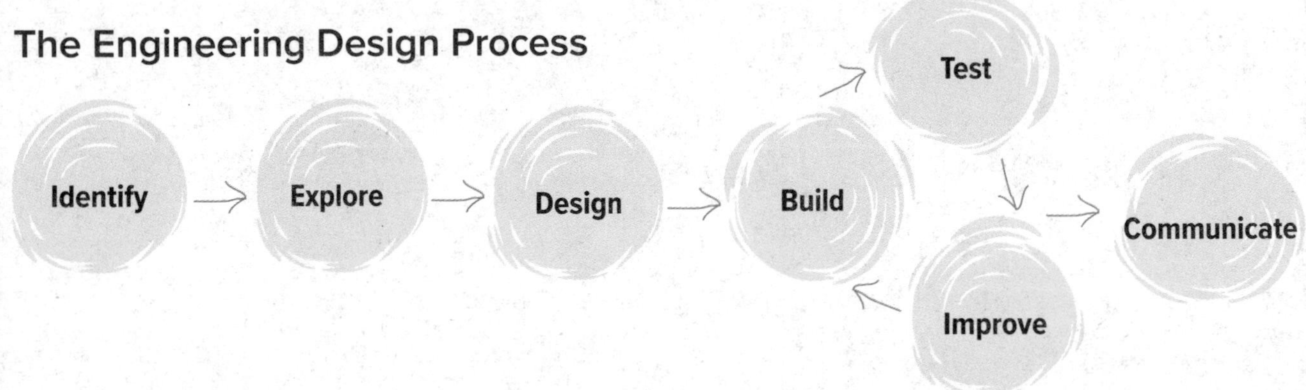

Build Your Model

Design Goals

1. Identify a problem caused by erosion and come up with at least two solutions on how to prevent it. You may want to research soil-erosion solutions that engineers have designed.
2. Determine the criteria for your models, and list the materials you will use to build your models.
3. Use your project planning to build your models.
4. Record the steps of your procedures to carry out fair tests of your models. Identify variables in each test.
5. Use the results of your test to compare your two models. Then select the design that best meets the criteria and constraints of the project.

Materials

Procedure:

Test Your Model

Build and test your models. Record your observations and results. Use a data table or separate piece of paper, if needed. Select the design that best meets the criteria, and present it to another group. Share your research, and provide feedback on each other's solutions.

You are using the Engineering Design Process!

PERFORMANCE EXPECTATION

STEM Module Project
Engineering Challenge

Communicate Your Results

Share the plan for your models and your results with another group. Compare how well each of your models was able to meet the criteria of withstanding the process of erosion. Discuss how well your models met the criteria and constraints, and ways you can improve your models. Communicate your findings below.

MODULE WRAP-UP

REVISIT THE PHENOMENON

Using what you learned in this module, explain how Earth's land features were formed.

How have your ideas changed? Explain your answer.

Earthquakes

Look at some of the damage caused by the 1989 Loma Prieta earthquake in San Francisco, CA!

Why do you think this building collapsed, but the others did not?

GO ONLINE
Watch the video *California Earthquakes* to see the phenomenon in action.

Talk About It

Look at the photo and watch the video of an earthquake causing a building to collapse. What questions do you have? Talk about them with a partner.

Did You Know?

About 50 earthquakes happen somewhere in the world each day. Each year, there are about 20,000 earthquakes worldwide!

STEM Module Project Launch

Engineering Challenge

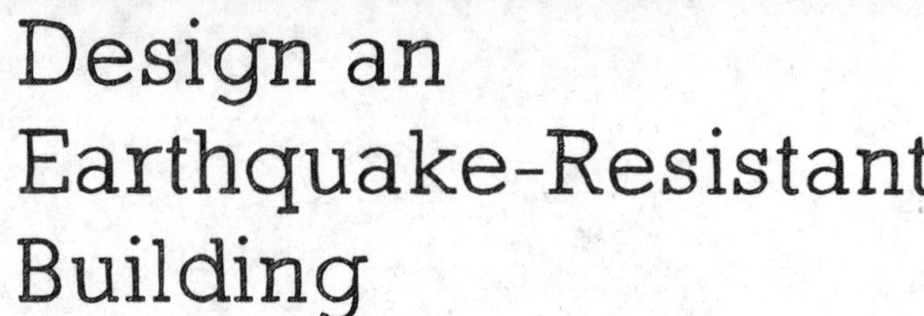

Design an Earthquake-Resistant Building

Lesson 1
Map Earthquakes

Lesson 2
Model Earthquake Movement

Lesson 3
Reduce Earthquake Damage

How do some buildings stay standing during an earthquake while others do not? At the end of this module, you will work with a small group to develop two designs for a school in California. You will design, build, and test two models of a school building to determine their ability to resist the forces of an earthquake. You will compare the test results of your two models and select the model that best minimizes earthquake damage.

Jane Horvath is a structural engineer. She uses her knowledge of materials, forces, and earth science to design safe structures. Structural engineers apply what they know to design structures that are safe.

FINN
Construction Manager

STEM Module Project

Plan and Complete the Engineering Challenge You will use what you learn to build and test your buildings!

LESSON 1 LAUNCH

Locations of Earthquakes

Two friends were talking about where earthquakes occur on Earth's surface. They wondered if earthquakes occur in a pattern. This is what they said:

Jerome: *I think earthquakes happen in a pattern near certain types of landforms on Earth's surface, like volcanoes, mountains, and ocean trenches.*

Anjali: *There is no pattern! Earthquakes happen all over the world and are random.*

Who do you agree with most? ______________________________

Explain why you agree.

____

____

____

____

You will revisit the Science Probe later in the lesson.

Map Earthquakes

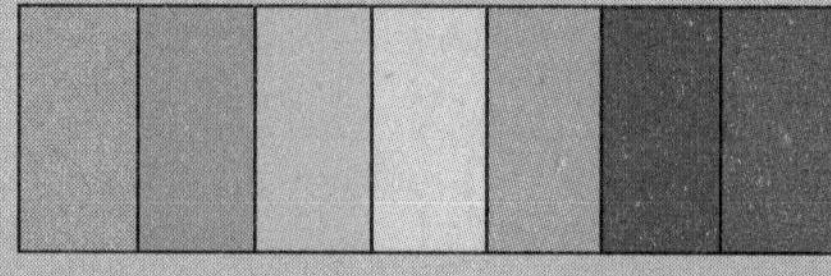

Potential Damage from an Earthquake Key

Lowest Hazard → Highest Hazard

ENCOUNTER
THE PHENOMENON

ESS2.B

Why are earthquakes more likely to occur in some places rather than others?

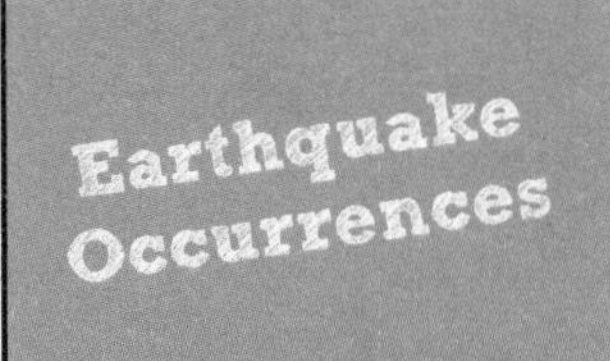

GO ONLINE

Watch the video *Earthquake Occurrences* to see the phenomenon in action.

Look at the map showing occurrences of earthquakes in the continental United States.

Talk About It

Circle the areas on the map that have the highest risk for earthquakes. Use the map's key to help you. What do you observe? Talk about your ideas with a partner. Record your thoughts below.

Did You Know?

Southern California experiences about 10,000 earthquakes a year! This is quite different from Ohio, where only about 200 earthquakes have been recorded since 1776.

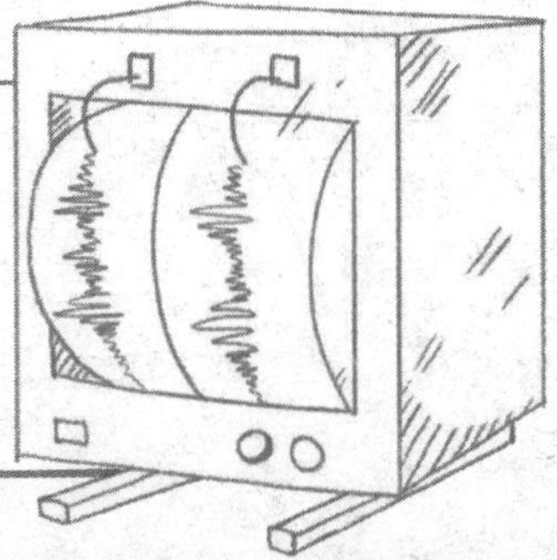

INQUIRY ACTIVITY

Data Analysis

Plot Earthquakes

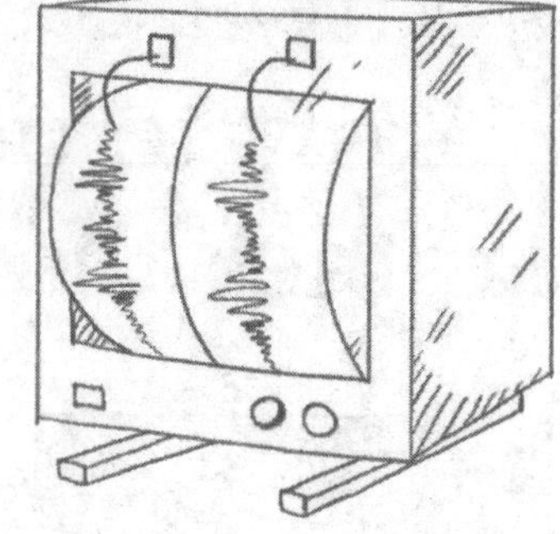

You have learned that an earthquake is a sudden movement of Earth's crust. Earthquakes occur all over the world. Is there a pattern to the occurrence of earthquakes? Look at the map of North America on the next page.

Make a Prediction Where in the continental United States do you think the majority of the strongest earthquakes occur?

Carry Out an Investigation

1. **MATH Connection** Use the table and map on the next page to plot the points, using the latitude and longitude for ten major earthquakes. Be sure to label each point you plot with the corresponding letter.
2. Describe any patterns you found in the locations of the earthquakes you plotted.

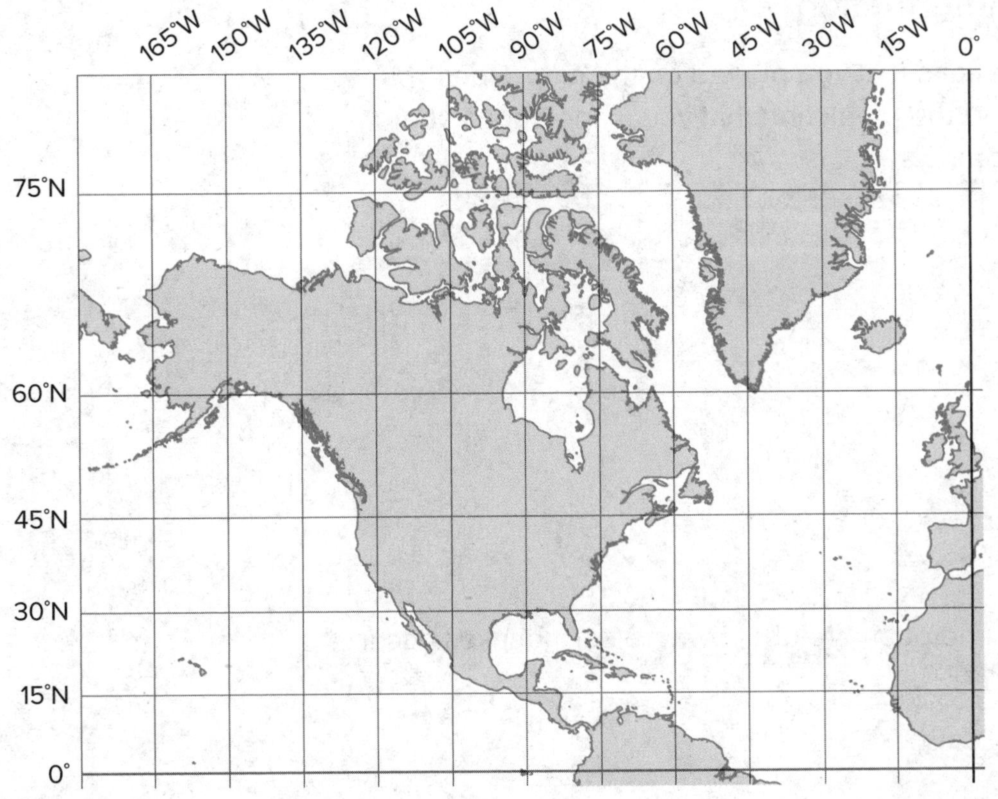

Earthquake Locations					
Earthquake	**Latitude**	**Longitude**	**Earthquake**	**Latitude**	**Longitude**
A	**37° N**	**122° W**	**F**	**41° N**	**125° W**
B	**69° N**	**147° W**	**G**	**14° N**	**118° W**
C	**36° N**	**120° W**	**H**	**40° N**	**125° W**
D	**1° N**	**79° W**	**I**	**60° N**	**152° W**
E	**37° N**	**118° W**	**J**	**48° N**	**121° W**

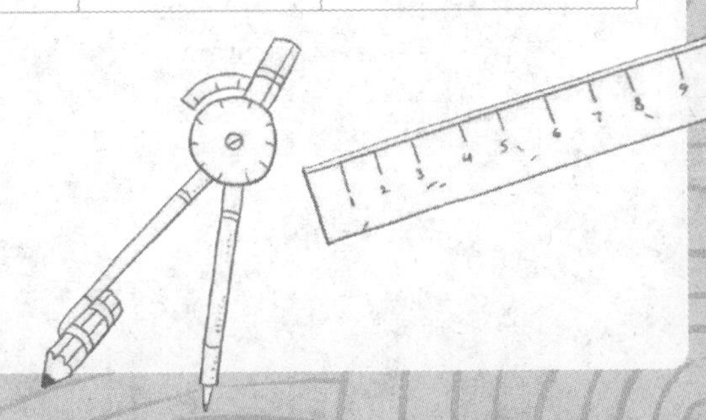

INQUIRY ACTIVITY

Communicate Information

3. Look at the locations that you plotted on the map. Does your evidence support the prediction that you made about where earthquakes occur?

4. How could you find out more about where earthquakes occur?

5. **MATH Connection** Think about how you could teach a younger student to do this activity. Explain how you plotted the points on the map using longitude and latitude.

MAKE YOUR CLAIM

Where do you think future earthquakes will occur?

Make a claim about where future earthquakes may occur.

CLAIM

I think future earthquakes will occur ________________.

Cite evidence from the activity.

EVIDENCE

The evidence I found in the *Plot Earthquakes* activity included that ________________.

Add reasoning for your claim, using what you know.

REASONING

My reasoning for my claim is ________________.

You will revisit your claim to add more evidence later in this lesson!

Earthquakes

VOCABULARY

Look for these words as you read:

fault

GO ONLINE Watch the video *Earthquake Mapping* to learn more about patterns of where earthquakes occur.

Earth's crust is made up of huge slabs of solid rock called plates that are always in motion. There are breaks or cracks where these plates come together. These cracks are called **faults**. In some places, Earth's plates can slide slowly past each other along a fault. In other places, plates can push together, move under or over each other, or even move apart from each other. This type of plate movement causes earthquakes to occur.

You have learned that earthquakes are movements in Earth's crust that are caused by a sudden shift of Earth's plates. The constant movement of Earth's plates puts stress on rock that is on both sides of a fault. As plates grind against each other, energy builds up in these rocks. When this energy is released, the crust shakes, vibrations reach Earth's surface, and an earthquake occurs.

The San Andreas Fault, located in California, is an area where many earthquakes occur. This fault line sits between a continental and oceanic boundary.

Patterns of Earth's Features

Below is a topographic map of the world. This map shows different landforms, such as mountain ranges and deep ocean trenches, which usually form along the boundary of two oceanic plates or an oceanic and continental plate. The map also outlines the continental boundaries and boundaries between continents and oceans. Many faults are located along these boundaries. As you investigated from the Inquiry Activity, *Plot Earthquakes*, most of the points you plotted on the map were along the plate boundary between North America and the Pacific Ocean. Think about the relationship between the earthquake locations you plotted and the locations of landforms and plate boundaries shown on the map below.

GO ONLINE Use the simulation *World Earthquakes and Volcanoes* to explore patterns in the location of earthquakes and volcanoes.

Talk About It

Discuss with a partner any patterns you observe in the locations of Earth's features and the locations of earthquakes.

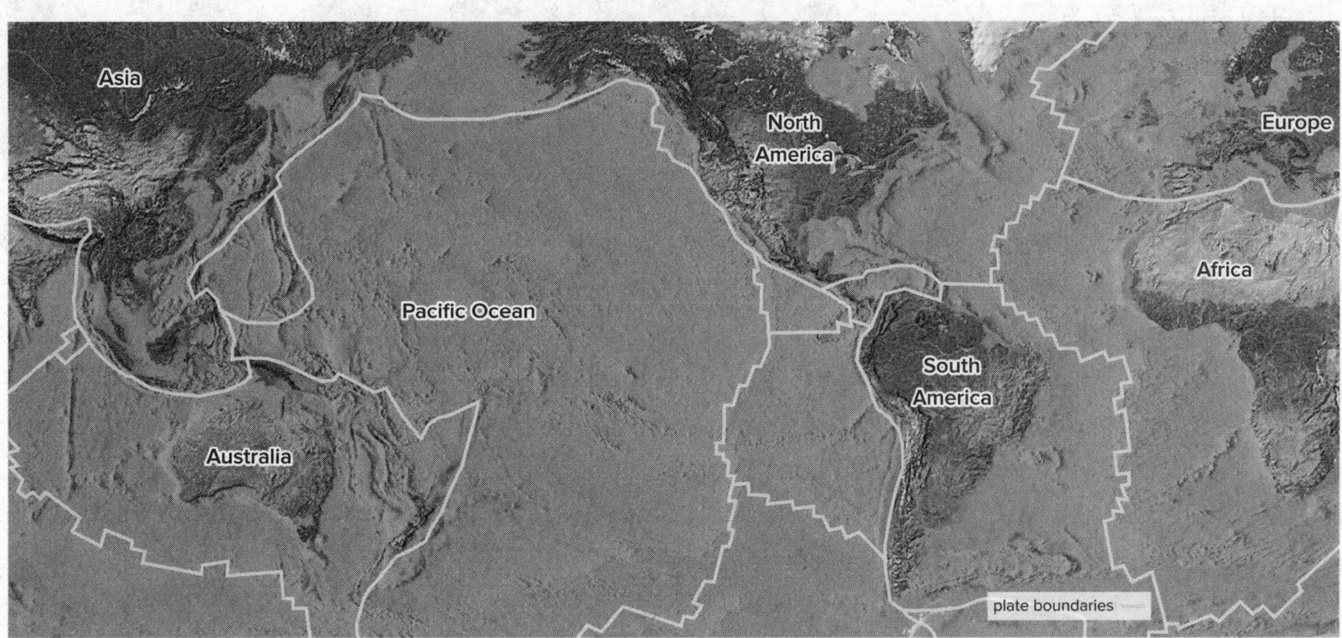

GO ONLINE Explore *Patterns on Earth's Surface* to learn more about mountain ranges, earthquakes, and volcanoes.

Inspect

Look at the map. What do you see?

Read the passage *Where Earthquakes Occur.* Circle text evidence that tells where earthquakes occur.

Find Evidence

Reread How do you know there is a pattern to where earthquakes occur?

Highlight the text evidence that supports your answer.

Notes

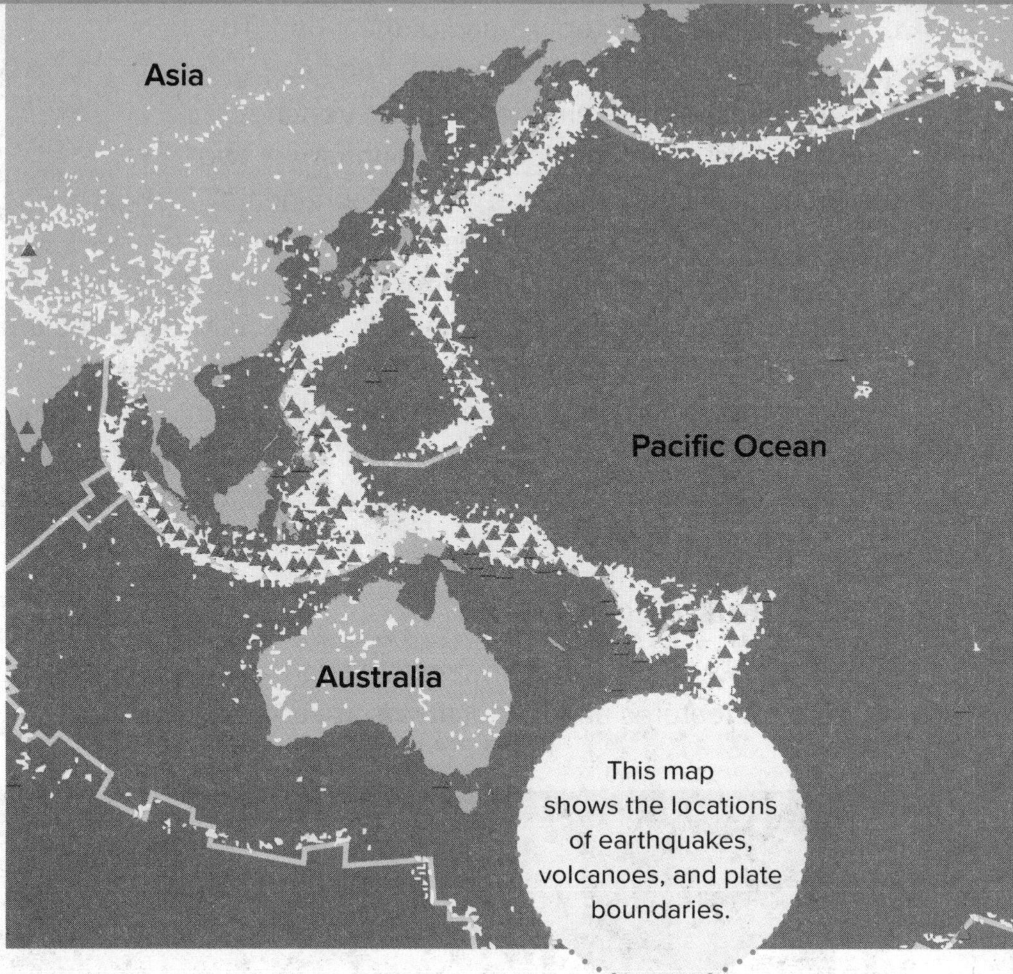

This map shows the locations of earthquakes, volcanoes, and plate boundaries.

Where Earthquakes Occur

Looking at the map above, you can see that most earthquakes happen along the edges of ocean and continental plate boundaries. There is an area around the Pacific Ocean where a number of Earth's plates meet. This area is known as the "Ring of Fire" because many earthquakes and volcanic eruptions occur here. If you compare this map to the topographic map on page 79, you can see that mountain ranges and deep ocean trenches are also found near or along continental and ocean plate boundaries. This pattern of earthquake locations helps seismologists, scientists who study earthquakes, to understand where earthquakes are likely to occur. However, it is difficult for seismologists to predict when an earthquake will occur.

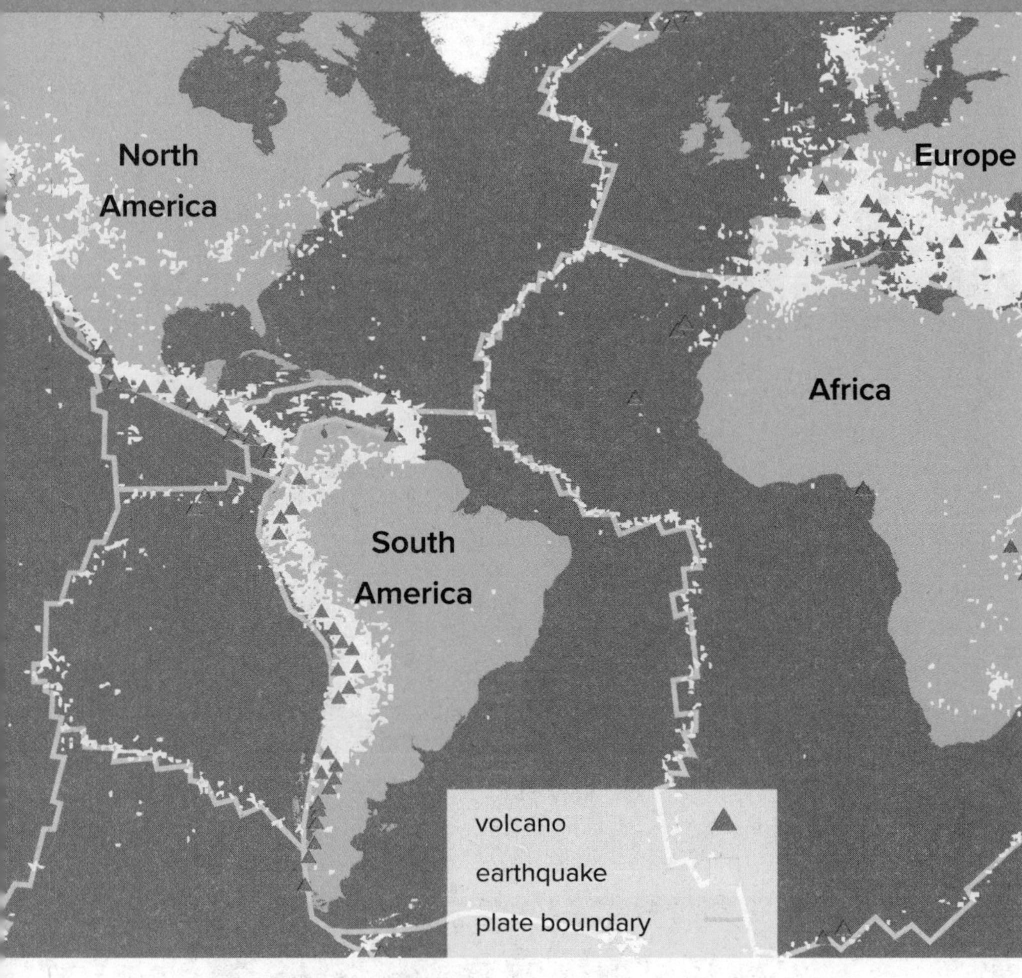

The San Andreas Fault in California runs along the boundary between the North American and the Pacific Ocean plates, where a number of earthquakes occur. Other areas, like California, experience many earthquakes. In these areas, seismologists monitor changes in the ground with the use of instruments that measure bulges or changes in the angle of the ground.

Label the San Andreas Fault on the map. How can you **analyze and interpret data** to explain a **pattern** in its **location**?

REVISIT Revisit the Page Keeley Science Probe from earlier in the lesson.

Make Connections

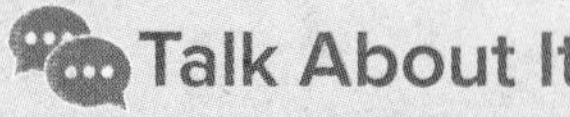

Talk About It

What do you think? Why might an engineer design a new tool for earthquake investigations?

Notes

STEM CAREER Connections

What Does a Cartographer Do?

Cartographers study landforms and create maps. They use several sources of data to create different types of maps. Cartographers usually gather data from the field. This means they will go to the place they are mapping rather than just use photos. They may also see changes in the land as construction or natural hazards occur.

Long ago, cartographers would draw maps by hand. While some may still use this method, now they can use computers and satellite images to draw interactive maps.

It's Your Turn

Think like a cartographer. Complete the activity on the next page. Explore the relationship between landforms and earthquakes.

Talk About It

How would a structural engineer benefit from the information from a cartographer?

INQUIRY ACTIVITY

Research

Earth's Features

You will investigate a pattern in the location of Earth's features and earthquakes.

Make a Prediction Is there a pattern in the location of landforms and where earthquakes occur?

Carry Out an Investigation

1. Use the topographic world map provided by your teacher. Cut along the boundary lines. There should be 16 pieces total.

2. Compare your completed puzzle to the maps on pages 79, 80, and 81. Look at where the boundaries come together in your puzzle. How does this relate to where earthquakes occur? What causes earthquakes?

ENVIRONMENTAL Connection

3. Based on the information you collected, explain why California has so many earthquakes. How do you think this affects life in California?

COLLECT EVIDENCE

Add evidence to your claim on page 77 about where earthquakes occur.

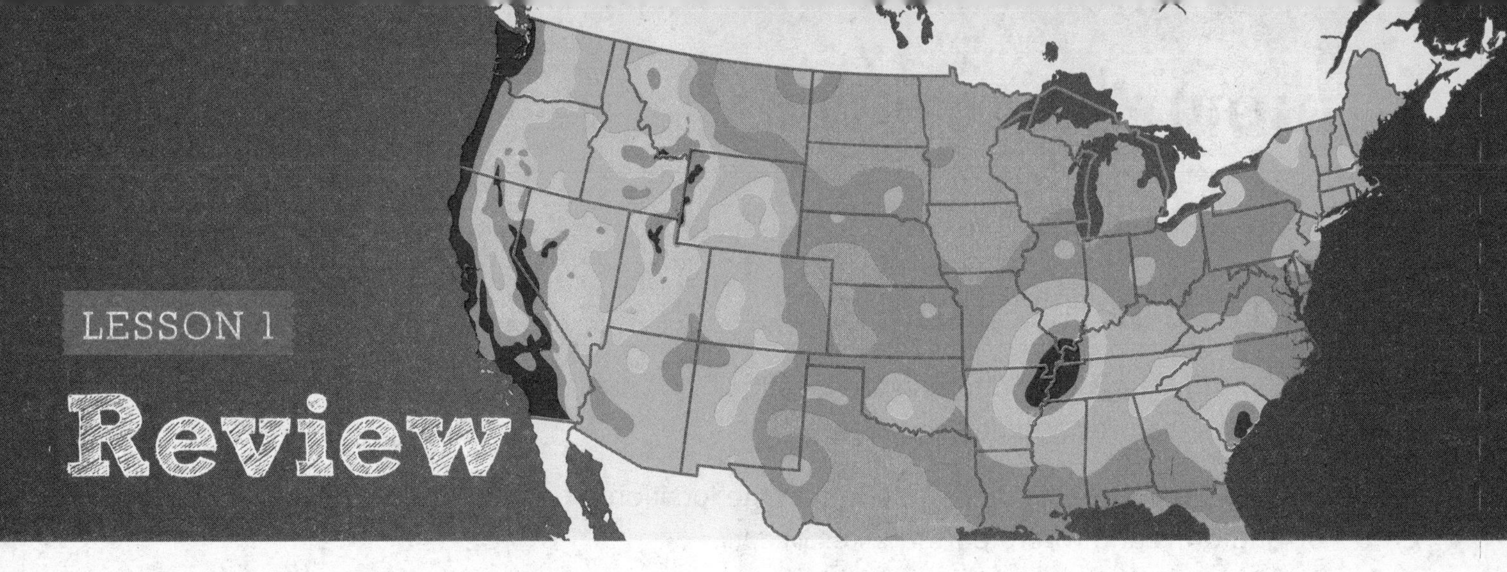

EXPLAIN THE PHENOMENON

Why are earthquakes more likely to occur in some places rather than others?

Summarize It

Explain why earthquakes are more likely to occur in some places than others, including in California.

Return to the Science Probe on page 71. Has your thinking changed? If so, explain.

Three-Dimensional Thinking

1. The map below shows Earth's crust broken into 12 major plates. These plates are in constant motion, and Earth experiences earthquakes every day.

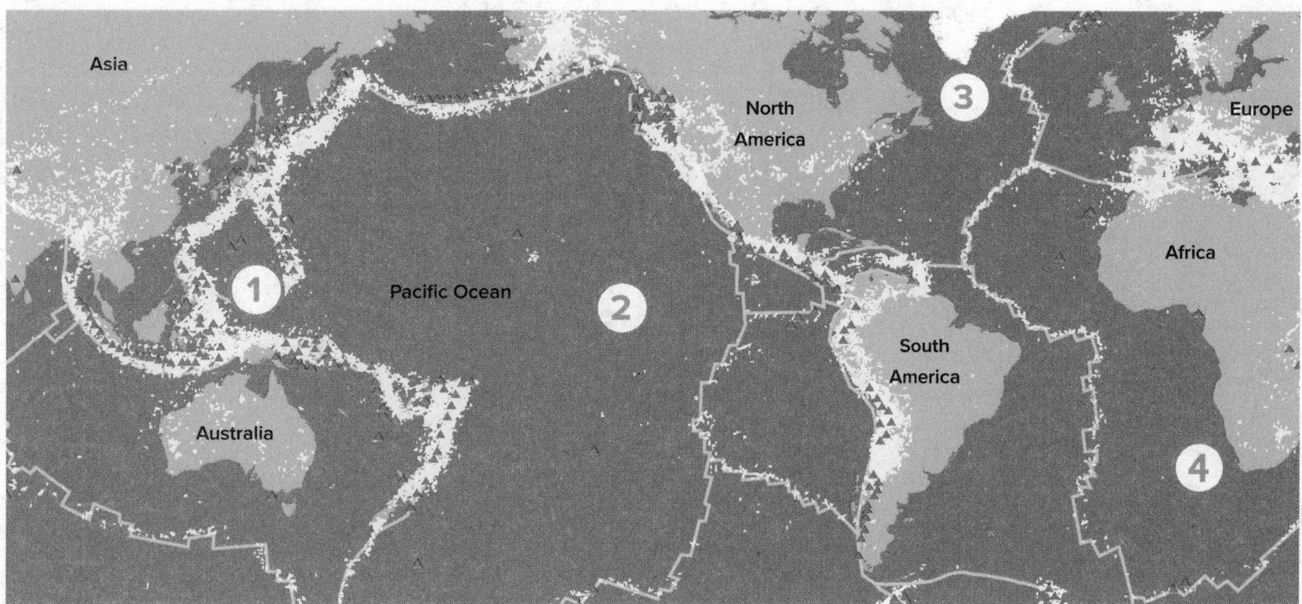

Think about patterns of earthquakes. Which number on the map shows where earthquakes are most likely to occur?

A. 1

B. 2

C. 3

D. 4

2. Looking at the map above, explain what you know about the pattern of where earthquakes occur.

Extend It

Use evidence from the lesson to support your opinion about whether or not homes in your area should have earthquake-resistant structures.

What questions do you still have about earthquakes?

Plan and carry out an investigation or research to find the answer to your question.

KEEP PLANNING

STEM Module Project

Engineering Challenge

You have learned where earthquakes occur. Go to your Module Project and explain how the information will affect your plan for your building.

SCIENCE PROBES

LESSON 2 LAUNCH

Ground-Shaking Event

Tania and Blanca's teacher invited a seismologist from the Southern California Earthquake Center to talk about earthquakes. After they listened to her speak, the two girls had different ideas about how earthquakes move. This is what they said:

Tania: *I think that all earthquakes have the same intensity and shake at the same speed.*

Blanca: *I think that earthquakes have different intensities and shake at different speeds.*

Whom do you agree with most? ______________________________

Explain why you agree.

____

____

____

____

____

You will revisit the Science Probe later in the lesson.

LESSON 2

Model Earthquake Movement

ENCOUNTER
THE PHENOMENON

How do water ripples model earthquake movement?

GO ONLINE

Watch the video *Water Drop* to see the phenomenon in action.

Talk About It

Look at the photo and watch the video of a water drop. What do you observe? Have you ever experienced this phenomenon before? Talk about your questions with a partner. Record your thoughts in the space below.

Did You Know?

Earthquakes travel in waves across the Earth and through the layers of Earth.

INQUIRY ACTIVITY

Hands On

Make Waves

Think back to the photo you saw at the beginning of the lesson. The drop of water produced small, gentle waves. A larger disturbance, like a speeding boat, would produce larger waves. What happens when waves reach objects floating in the water? In this activity, you will observe the effects that different types and sizes of waves have on objects.

Make a Prediction Will the waves move the objects to a different position? Explain your answer.

Materials

- aluminum pan with water
- ruler
- cork
- spring toy
- modeling clay
- masking tape

Carry Out an Investigation

1. Fill the pan with water to a depth of 2.5 cm. Place the cork in the middle of the pan and wait until the cork stops moving.
2. Gently move the pan back and forth once or twice.
3. **Record Data** Record observations of the motion and final position of the cork in the data table.
4. Move the pan back and forth a little harder this time to create larger waves. Observe and record the motion and final position of the cork.
5. Clear your workspace. Using the spring toy, attach a small piece of modeling clay near the center of it. Mark the position of the clay on your workspace with a piece of tape.
6. Have a partner hold one end of the spring toy while you hold the other. Stretch the spring slightly so there is some tension. On your workspace surface, use two pieces of tape to mark the ends of the stretched spring toy.

7. Create several small pulses by repeatedly stretching the spring and returning the spring to its original position. Record observations of the motion and position of the clay once the waves stop.

8. Create larger pulses by repeatedly stretching the spring and returning the spring to its original position. Record your observations.

Observations		
	Motion	**Final Position**
Water/Cork— Small Waves		
Cork— Large Waves		
Spring/Clay— Small Waves		
Clay— Large Waves		

INQUIRY ACTIVITY

Communicate Information

9. How did the different waves move the objects? What patterns of motion did you notice?

10. Do your results support your prediction? How did the waves affect the movement of the cork and modeling clay?

Talk About It

Discuss with your partner what causes wave movement, and how it is similar to earthquake movement.

MAKE YOUR CLAIM

How do the waves in the investigation compare to the waves produced by an earthquake?

Make a claim.

CLAIM

Cite evidence from this lesson.

EVIDENCE

Give reasoning for your claim, using what you know.

REASONING

You will revisit your claim to add more evidence later in this lesson.

VOCABULARY

Look for these words as you read:

amplitude

magnitude

seismic wave

seismograph

transverse wave

wavelength

Waves

What do the waves that you just modeled have to do with earthquakes? Earthquakes produce waves. Think back to the lesson phenomenon. The drop disturbed the surface when it hit the still water. The disturbance produced a series of circles that grew larger as they moved away from the center. These circles are waves. Recall that a wave is a disturbance that transfers energy from one point to another. Just like the drop of water, earthquakes produce waves that ripple outward from the place where the disturbance begins. The sudden movement of an earthquake causes rocks to vibrate. A vibration that travels through Earth and is produced by an earthquake is called a **seismic wave**. Seismic waves spread out in all directions from the focus, the point where an earthquake begins.

The movement of particles by waves is called vibration. Waves are classified by the type of vibration they cause in materials. Longitudinal waves, such as sound waves, move materials back and forth as the wave travels through it. You used the spring toy to produce longitudinal waves. A **transverse wave** is a wave that vibrates perpendicular to the direction that the energy moves. Transverse waves move material up and down as they travel. Earthquakes produce both longitudinal and transverse waves.

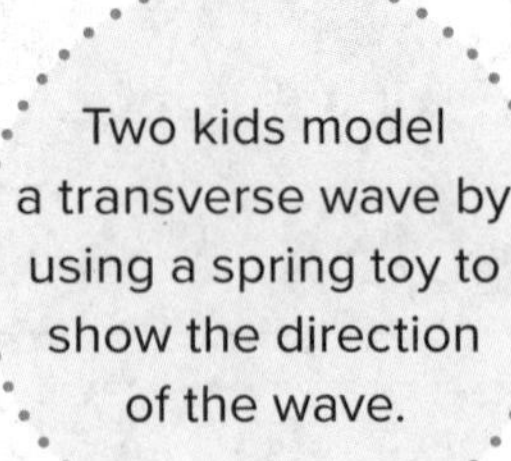

Two kids model a transverse wave by using a spring toy to show the direction of the wave.

1. In what ways could you use a spring to model a transverse wave? A longitudinal wave?

Features of Waves

The crest of a transverse wave is its highest point. In a longitudinal wave, it is the point where the particles are closest together. Waves also have troughs. The trough of a transverse wave is its lowest point. In a longitudinal wave, it is the point where the particles are farthest apart. For example, the highest point of an ocean wave is the crest, and the lowest point is the trough. Consider a boat on the water. As a wave goes by, the boat rises with the crest and falls with the trough. The boat moves up and down with the wave motion but it doesn't really move in any direction, except when it is close to the shoreline. **Wavelength** is the distance between wave crests or troughs. *Frequency* is the measure of how many crests or troughs move through a given point in one unit of time. High-frequency waves have shorter wavelengths and transfer more energy. The frequency and speed of a wave are not the same. The speed of a wave depends on the material through which it travels.

Amplitude is the height of a wave from its crest or trough to its midpoint. It is a measure of the wave's strength.

PRIMARY SOURCE

Scientists working on the ShakeAlert Earthquake Early Warning System. This system will help keep people safe when the next big earthquake occurs on the West Coast.

All waves transfer energy without permanently moving the material through which they travel. This means that after a wave has passed, particles end up in about the same position they started in.

2. Draw waves with the characteristics indicated below.

Long wavelength, low frequency:

Short wavelength, high frequency:

Label a Diagram: Parts of Waves

Use what you learned to label the wavelength, amplitude, crest, and trough of each wave.

GO ONLINE Watch the video *Earthquake Movement* to see how earthquake waves move.

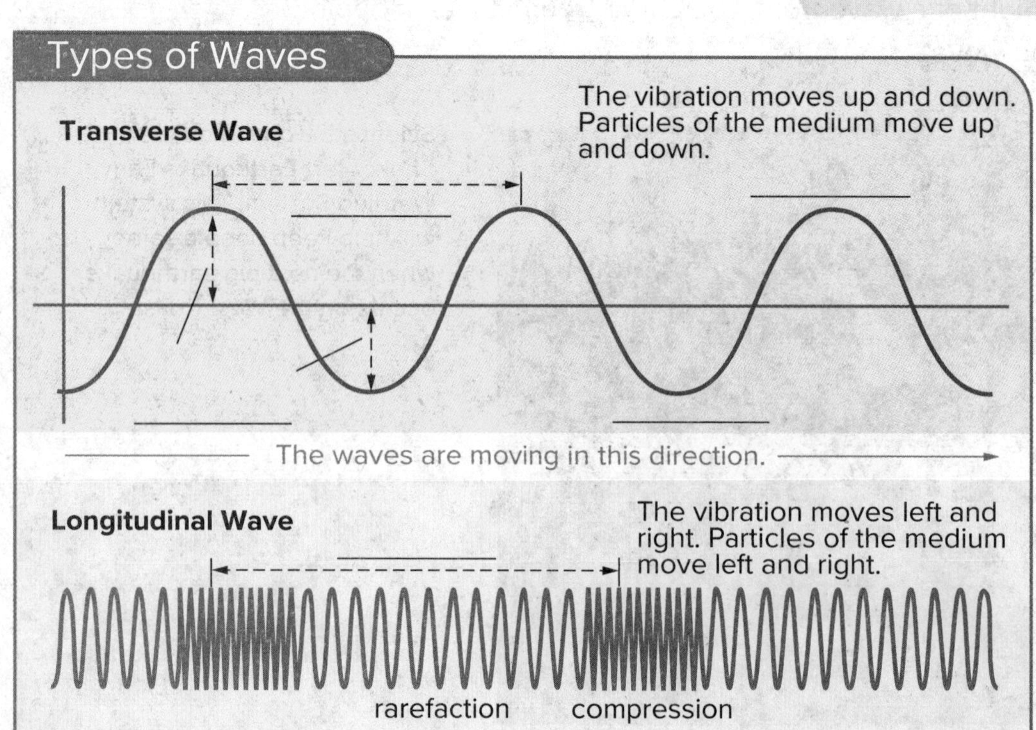

Record and Measure Earthquakes

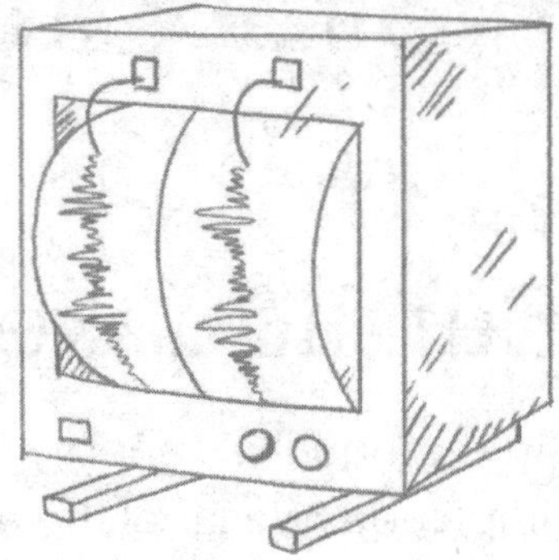

Scientists measure seismic waves with a seismograph. A **seismograph** is an instrument used to detect and record earthquakes. The device shows the waves as curvy lines. The stronger the quake, the steeper the lines.

The amount of energy released by an earthquake is its **magnitude**. The Richter scale measures magnitude, the largest ground movement, when an earthquake occurs. It rates earthquakes from weakest to strongest starting at 1. Each larger whole number indicates that an earthquake has released 32 times more energy.

The Mercalli scale measures what people felt and what happened during an earthquake. It uses Roman numerals from I to XII.

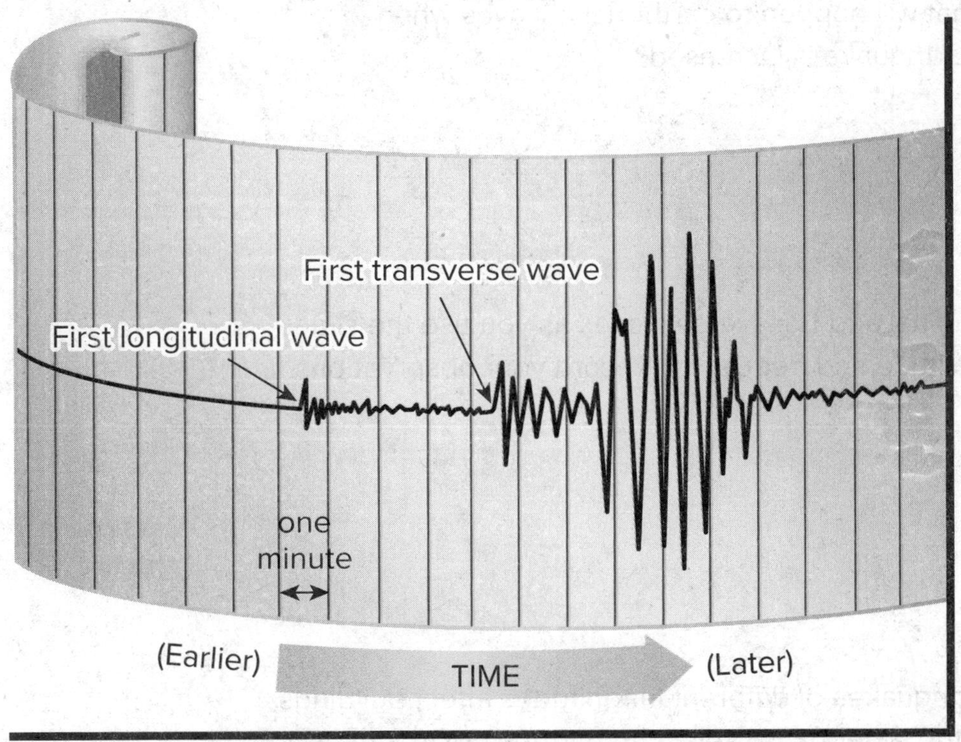

3. What do you think happens to the amplitude of an earthquake wave when its magnitude increases?

INQUIRY ACTIVITY

Simulation

Earthquake Waves

An earthquake's energy is determined by the wave's frequency and amplitude. We label the amount of energy an earthquake's wave has as magnitude.

Earthquake Waves

Use the simulation *Earthquake Waves* to complete the activity.

Now you will observe earthquakes of different magnitudes and see how they move the ground and buildings.

Make a Prediction What will happen to earthquake waves when the magnitude of the earthquake is increased?

1. Observe the longitudinal and transverse waves as you use the slider to change their amplitude and frequency. Record your observations.

2. Investigate how earthquakes of different magnitudes affect buildings on Solid Rock. Use the slider bar to select an earthquake magnitude. Press the play button to set off the earthquake.
3. **Record Data** Test magnitudes 2, 4, 6, and 8. Use the camera button to take a picture of the effects for each of these magnitudes. Record your data in the table.
4. Repeat steps 2–3 to investigate the effects of earthquakes on buildings on Soil.

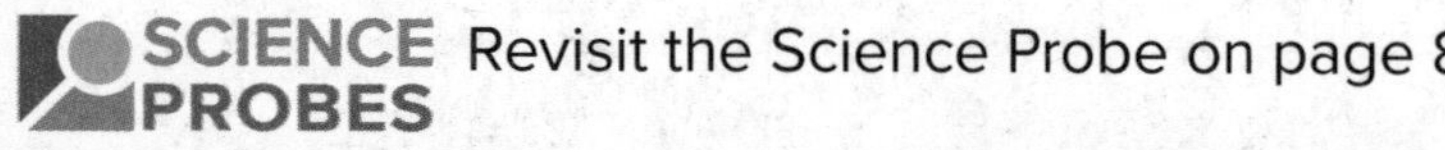

Revisit the Science Probe on page 87.

Observations				
Magnitude	Solid Rock		Soil	
	building	seismograph	building	seismograph
2				
4				
6				
8				

Using the notebook in the simulation, explain how you can **develop and use a model** to describe **patterns** of a wave's amplitude and wavelength. Use a drawing to support your response.

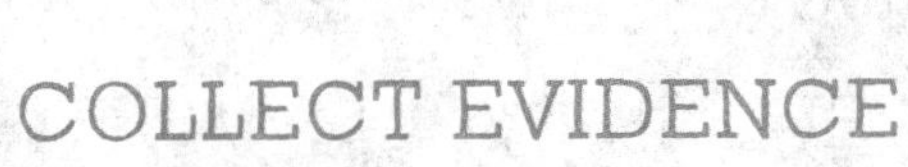

COLLECT EVIDENCE

Use your observations as evidence to add to your claim in the table on page 93.

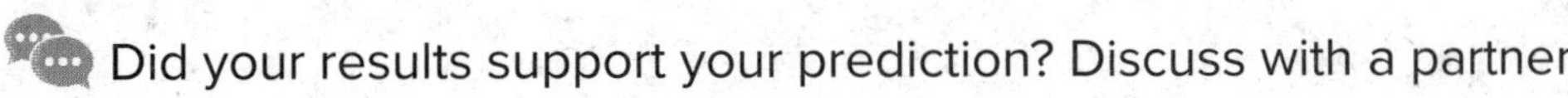

Did your results support your prediction? Discuss with a partner.

STEM CAREER Connection

How Could You Become a Seismologist?

Do you wonder how you can reduce the effects of an earthquake? If so, then seismology might be the field for you. Seismographs record the waves produced by earthquakes. **Seismologists** study these waves to look for patterns.

Seismologists study seismic waves and their effects on Earth in the past and the present. The black and white photos show the effect of an earthquake that occurred in Kern County in 1952. Seismologists use this data to help engineers design buildings that can better withstand the shaking caused by earthquakes.

Seismologists work with computers and other tools to collect and analyze data. Seismologists often find work in the petroleum industry, in government organizations, and at universities.

1952 Kern County earthquake

It's Your Turn

Like a seismologist, you will now analyze data from past earthquakes. Complete the activity on the next page to find out more about earthquakes of different strengths.

Historical Earthquakes in California

California has experienced a great number of earthquakes throughout its history. On a separate sheet of graph paper, plot the points in the table. Analyze and interpret your data to answer the questions below.

PRIMARY SOURCE

1994 Northridge earthquake

California Earthquake Data					
Year	**Location**	**Magnitude**	**Year**	**Location**	**Magnitude**
1906	**San Francisco**	**7.8**	**1980**	**West of Eureka**	**7.2**
1911	**Calaveras Fault**	**6.5**	**1984**	**Morgan Hill**	**6.2**
1920	**Los Angeles**	**4.9**	**1989**	**Loma Prieta**	**6.9**
1923	**Off Cape Mendocino**	**7.2**	**1992**	**Landers**	**7.3**
1933	**Long Beach**	**6.4**	**1994**	**Northridge**	**6.7**
1940	**Imperial Valley**	**7.1**	**2004**	**Parkfield**	**6.0**
1954	**East of Arcata**	**6.6**	**2010**	**Baja California**	**7.2**

1. According to the data, which decade experienced the most earthquakes?

2. What patterns can you identify in the intensity of past earthquakes?

EXPLAIN THE PHENOMENON

How do water ripples model earthquake movement?

Summarize It!

Use what you have learned to explain how the movement of water ripples is like the movement of earthquake waves.

Return to the Science Probe on page 87. Has your thinking changed? If so, explain how it has changed.

Three-Dimensional Thinking

1. What factors affect the speed of a wave?

2. ______________ move material back and forth.

   A. Transverse waves

   B. Longitudinal waves

   C. Wavelengths

   D. None of the above

3. Why is it important to know the magnitude of an earthquake?

4. **MATH Connection** If a seismometer records an earthquake of 7.0 magnitude, how much energy is released compared to a 6.0 earthquake?

Extend It

You are a builder in your community. How might you communicate with the citizens about the effects of seismic waves on their homes?

Write a speech, draw a poster, create a flyer, or use media. Use the space below to write a draft.

What questions do you still have about seismic waves?

Plan and carry out an investigation or research to find the answer to your question.

KEEP PLANNING

STEM Module Project
Engineering Challenge

Now that you have learned about earthquake movement, go to your Module Project to explain how the information will affect your plan for your building.

SCIENCE PROBES

LESSON 3 LAUNCH

Shake, But Don't Fall

Earthquakes can cause man-made structures to collapse. Put a circle around the boxes that are examples of factors that could reduce earthquake damage.

Designing buildings that can resist forces from the side.	Building only in areas where there has been no record of earthquakes.	Reducing the height of buildings in areas where earthquakes are most likely to occur.
Making the frame of a building less heavy by reducing the number of beams.	Connecting beams and columns with diagonal pieces.	Training people to seek shelter under doorways.
Adding fluids deep into the ground to prevent earthquakes from occurring.	Preparing for earthquakes by paying close attention to the weather.	Raising the floor of houses above ground when building near coastlines.

Explain your choices.

You will revisit the Science Probe later in the lesson.

LESSON 3

Reduce Earthquake Damage

The original Oakland Bay Bridge was the longest bridge in the world when it opened in 1936.

ENCOUNTER
THE PHENOMENON

ESS3.B, ETS1.A, ETS1.B, ETS1.C

What features make structures resistant to earthquakes?

GO ONLINE

Watch the video *Bridges* to see the phenomenon in action.

Look at the photo and watch the video of the old and new eastern span of the Oakland Bay Bridge. What questions do you have about the phenomenon? Share your thoughts with a partner. Record or illustrate your thoughts below.

Did You Know?

The new eastern span of the Oakland Bay Bridge is suspended by one main cable made of 17,399 compressed wires. It's one of the largest spans of its kind in the world!

INQUIRY ACTIVITY

Hands On

Earthquake Effects

You have learned about how earthquake waves move.

Make a Prediction What effect does the motion from earthquakes have on roads and buildings?

Materials

tape

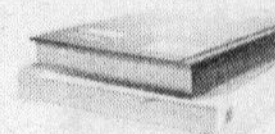
2 identical textbooks

construction paper

colored pencils

blocks

4 smooth pencils

Carry Out an Investigation

1. Tape a piece of construction paper to the cover of each textbook.
2. Place the books next to each other on a desk, spine to spine. Place two smooth, round pencils under each book, spaced so the books roll easily. Draw a "road" that crosses from one piece of construction paper to the other.
3. Use the blocks to construct a small "house" where the books meet.
4. Slowly and gently shake the desk to model an earthquake.
5. Record your observations by drawing a sketch and labeling the details of what you observed.
6. Line up the road and rebuild your house to match its appearance in step 3.
7. Shake the desk rapidly and with more force. Observe what happens to the road and the house.

8. Record your observations by drawing a sketch and labeling the details of what happened.

Communicate Information

9. What effect did the motion have on the roads and building? Use evidence to explain whether the results support your prediction.

How do you think you could keep the **structure** of your house and road from breaking? Draw a diagram to **design a solution** for how this would work.

Talk About It

What can be done to prevent earthquake damage? How could earthquakes damage a bridge? Share your ideas with a small group.

VOCABULARY

Look for these words as you read:

bracing

lateral force

shear wall

Predict Earthquakes

Most earthquakes are too weak to be noticed. Others cause extreme damage. During a major earthquake, buildings and roads might break apart. Bridges might collapse.

Seismologists use seismometers to identify and map the epicenters of earthquakes. Then they compare the epicenter location to known fault locations. They use this information to describe how rock along the faults has moved over time. They watch faults to let people know about the threat of possible earthquakes.

An earthquake damaged this highway.

1. Why would seismologists watch faults?

Earthquake Signs

A bulge or change in the angle of the ground is a sign that an earthquake is likely to occur. But even with these signs, it is difficult to predict how soon an earthquake will occur. It could be hours, days, weeks, or months before enough energy builds up for the ground to shift.

New technology can warn people that an earthquake is coming. The warning gives people notice of the arrival of an earthquake in seconds or minutes. This technology works by first detecting longitudinal waves from a break at a fault. The sensors then analyze the data to determine the location and size of the earthquake. The system sends a message stating the intensity and arrival time of the earthquake.

Label a Diagram: Earthquake Warning

Recall the information from Lesson 2 about how seismographs record seismic waves. Label the longitudinal wave and transverse wave in the diagram.

Earthquake Early Warning Basics

1. In an earthquake, longitudinal waves move the fastest. Transverse waves arrive later but cause more damage.

2. Sensors detect the longitudinal wave and transmit data to the earthquake alert center to determine the location and size of the quake.

3. A message is sent to your electronic device, which calculates the expected intensity and arrival time of the earthquake at your location.

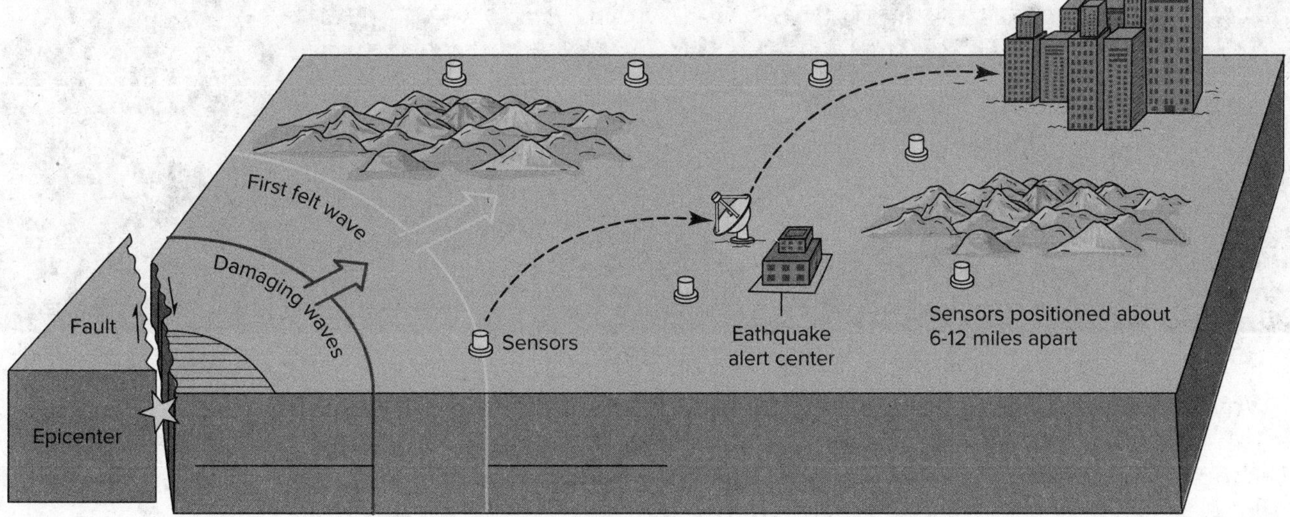

Earthquake Safety

You can stay safe during an earthquake by following a few simple rules. If you are indoors, duck under a table or doorway. Keep away from walls and windows. If you are outdoors, stay away from trees, power lines, and any structures that might fall down.

People cannot stop an earthquake from occurring, but they can take steps to reduce the damage it causes. Secure objects in your house that might fall if you live in an earthquake-prone area. You can also identify safe places to use as shelter during an earthquake.

Many of the objects in this house were moved or broken during the earthquake.

1. Why should you get under a sturdy table to stay safe in an earthquake?

Safe Structures

The building materials used can help a structure stand up to earthquakes. Materials such as bricks and concrete blocks crumble easily when shaken. Reinforced concrete, metal, and wood work better because they can be tied to other parts of the structure and do not crumble.

Shorter buildings might be less likely to be damaged in an earthquake, but tall buildings can also remain stable during an earthquake. Very tall buildings are more flexible than shorter buildings. Buildings that are more flexible are less likely to collapse.

Placing layers of rubber and steel, or motion dampeners, at the base of bridges can reduce damage from earthquakes. Some of these motion dampeners act like the shock absorbers in a car. Sections of bridges can be joined by rubber joints that allow the bridge to sway during an earthquake. The rubber joints make bridges more flexible.

Another safety feature can be seen in the east span of the Oakland Bay Bridge. It is suspended by a single cable from a main tower. The main tower is made up of four concrete towers designed to flex and remain intact through the strongest earthquakes.

Reinforced concrete has metal pieces inside that tie it together and keep it from breaking with movement.

This new Oakland Bay Bridge is more like a swing. Its single cable loops under the road and over its main tower.

2. How can a structure be more earthquake-resistant? Name two ways.

Inspect

Read this passage from the Investigator article *Designing Strong Buildings*.

Circle text evidence that tells you how bracing supports an earthquake-resistant building. Share your findings with a partner.

Find Evidence

Reread Find evidence in the text that the author thinks that buildings can resist lateral forces.

Reread How did the photos help the reader understand the author's message? Share your findings with a partner.

Notes

Designing Strong Buildings

Architects and scientists study earthquakes to design safe buildings. A building needs to resist lateral forces during an earthquake. **Lateral forces** are forces that come from the side. Buildings have steel, wood, or concrete frames. Horizontal beams support the weight of roofs and floors.

Beams transfer forces to vertical columns. Columns transfer forces to the foundation. The foundation transfers forces to the ground. The frame of a building can resist lateral forces with bracing. **Bracing** is made of diagonal pieces connecting beams and columns. Bracing comes in several shapes. Some bracing looks like the letter X. Other bracing looks like the letter K.

This building's frame has X bracing. Bracing can also look like the letter K.

This skyscraper in Taiwan was designed to withstand earthquakes.

Buildings can also resist lateral forces with shear walls. A **shear wall** is a stiff wall made of braced panels. Some tall buildings have a shear core. A shear core is usually a stairwell or elevator shaft with a shear wall on each side. Architects and engineers determine the size of a shear wall based on their calculations of potential lateral forces.

Another way for very tall buildings to resist lateral forces is with a damper. The damper is a mass that can weigh over a million pounds. It is attached to the building on the inside of the top floors. It moves independently from the building. This makes the building move less from lateral forces.

1. How do bracing and shear walls help a building?

This building has a 728-ton damper that helps it resist movement. The damper hangs between the 87th and 92nd floors.

GO ONLINE Watch the video *Earthquake Damage* to see more earthquake-resistant building features.

Revisit the Science Probe on page 105.

Make Connections

Talk About It

What is the author's point of view on the topic of buildings? What in the text makes you say that?

Notes

STEM CAREER Connections

Emergency Management Specialist

This emergency management specialist is helping people that were impacted by an earthquake.

Have you ever been in an emergency? Who helped you? Where did you go to stay safe? You might have been helped by a police officer or a medical doctor—there are many types of people who help in an emergency. But what if this emergency involved a natural disaster like an earthquake? That is where you would receive help from me! I am an **emergency management specialist** and I help people during emergencies, like earthquakes, tsunamis, and floods.

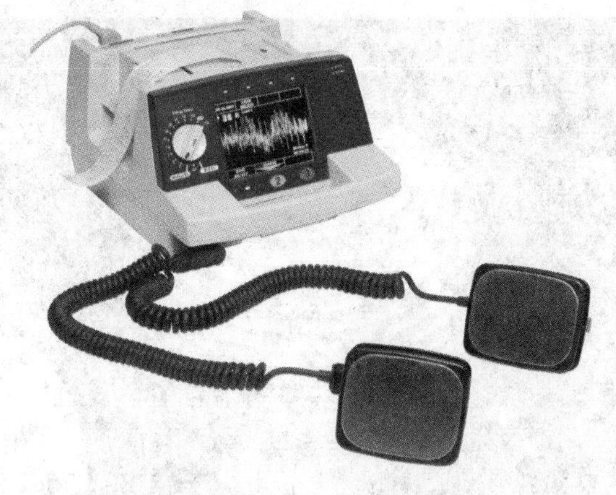

It is so rewarding to help people in need! Today I helped coordinate the delivery of food, water, and medicine to the victims of an earthquake in southern California. I also helped to set up shelters for those who had lost their homes. The victims were so grateful for help.

Not every day is as eventful as today, but we are constantly preparing for days like this. Sometimes I review emergency evacuation routes to make sure they are the most efficient. I help organize emergency response teams to respond quickly when natural disasters occur. I also help communities that have been hit by a natural disaster apply for emergency funds.

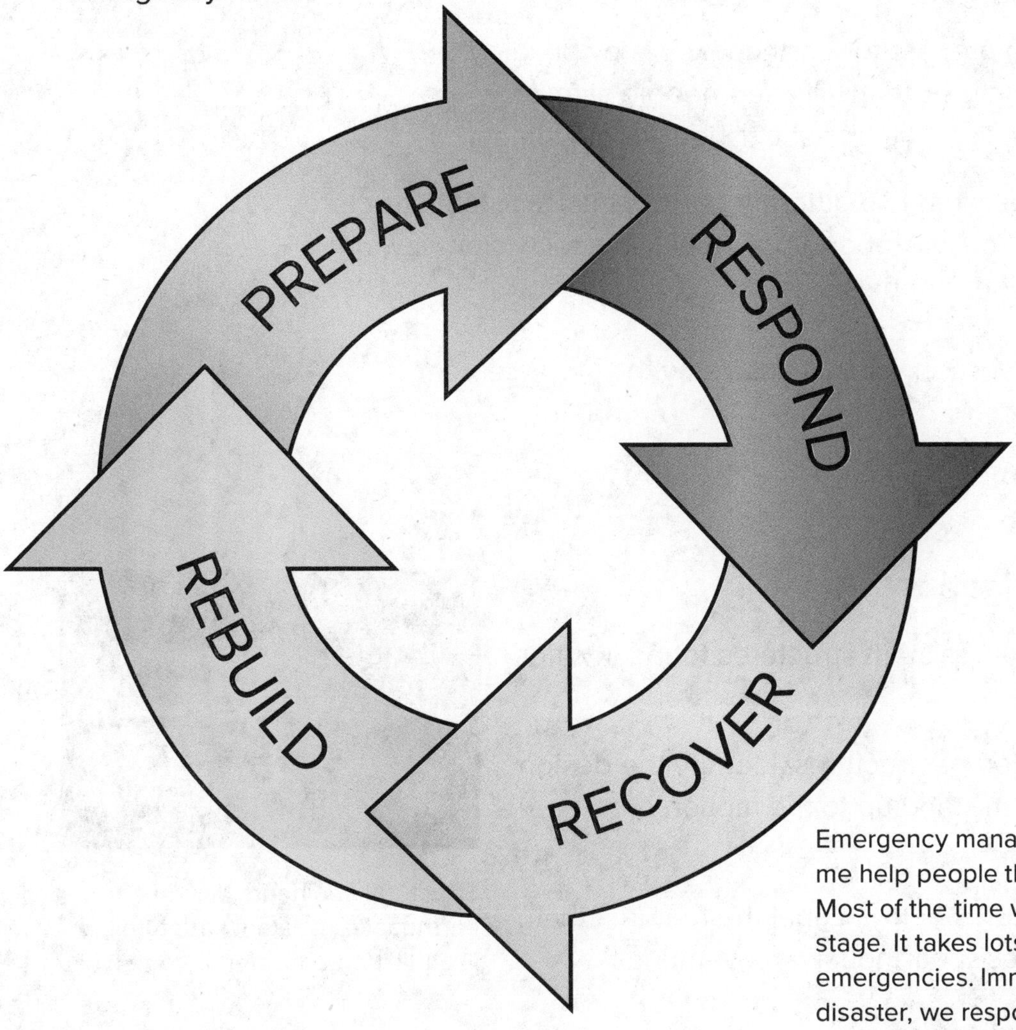

PREPARE

RESPOND

RECOVER

REBUILD

Emergency management specialists like me help people throughout an emergency. Most of the time we are in the preparing stage. It takes lots of planning to prepare for emergencies. Immediately after a natural disaster, we respond. In the days and months following, we help the people recover and then rebuild.

It's Your Turn

Think like an emergency management specialist. Complete the activity on the next page to research additional ways to reduce earthquake damage in your community.

Talk About It

How would an emergency management specialist help prepare for future earthquakes?

INQUIRY ACTIVITY

Research

Earthquake-Resistant Structures

One way that people can prepare for earthquakes is by building earthquake-resistant structures that will keep people safe. How are the buildings near you designed to resist earthquake movement?

In this activity, you will research two different earthquake-resistant structures found in cities near you. You will report your results in a television news story about how the designs keep us safe.

Ask a Question What question will you answer with your research?

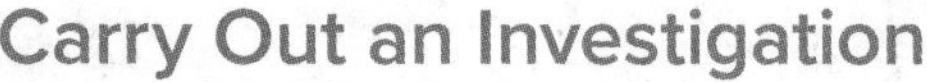

Carry Out an Investigation

1. Select two earthquake-resistant structures found in cities near you.
2. Research the two different structures. Identify the design features that help them stand up to the motion of an earthquake.
3. Sketch the two structures below. Label the features that help each structure resist earthquake movement.

Structural engineers design earthquake-resistant structures like this treated water storage tank.

4. How does each of the design features keep people safe?

5. How do the two structures compare?

6. Use your research to prepare a news story to present to the class. Be sure to use visuals to help explain your results. Use the space below to plan your presentation.

What do the **structure and function** of your design features have in common with earthquake-resistant buildings near you? Use evidence from your research to **construct your explanation**.

Talk About It

What other features would you invent to improve the chances of a structure resisting an earthquake? Share your thoughts with a partner.

EXPLAIN THE PHENOMENON

What features make structures resistant to earthquakes?

Summarize It

Explain how structures can be designed to reduce earthquake damage.

REVISIT

Return to the Science Probe on page 105. Has your thinking changed? If so, explain how it has changed.

Three-Dimensional Thinking

1. What patterns did you notice in earthquake-resistant structures?

2. How does knowing about earthquake waves help engineers design safer structures in a lab?

3. ______________ is made of diagonal pieces connecting beams and columns. It comes in several shapes.

   A. A lateral wall

   B. A damper

   C. A shear wall

   D. Bracing

Extend It

You are an emergency management specialist in your community. How might you communicate with your citizens about proper precautions to reduce earthquake damage?

Write a speech, draw a poster, create a flyer, or use media.

KEEP PLANNING

STEM Module Project

Engineering Challenge

Now that you have learned about reducing earthquake damage, go to your Module Project to explain how the information will affect your plan for your building.

STEM Module Project
Engineering Challenge

Design an Earthquake-Resistant Building

You've been hired as a structural engineer. Using what you have learned throughout this module, you will develop two designs for a school in California. Your goal will be to work with a small group to design, build, and test your models of a school building to see if they are able to resist the forces of an earthquake. You will compare the results of the test and select the design that best minimizes earthquake damage.

Planning after Lesson 1

Apply what you have learned about earthquakes and where they occur to your project planning.

How does knowing where earthquakes occur affect your project planning?

Record information to help you plan your model after each lesson.

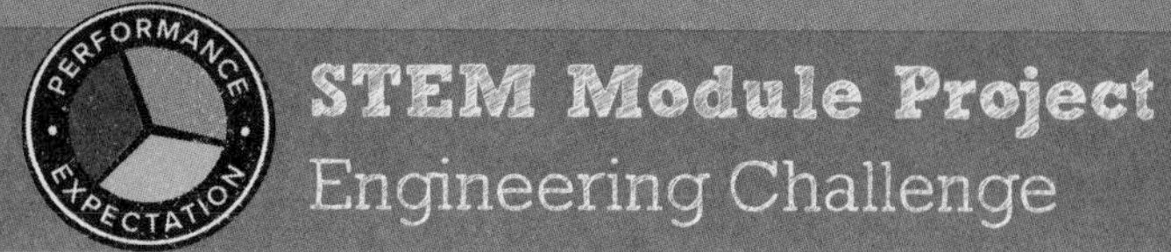

STEM Module Project
Engineering Challenge

Planning after Lesson 2

Apply what you learned about how earthquakes move to your project planning.

What factors should be considered when building your models?

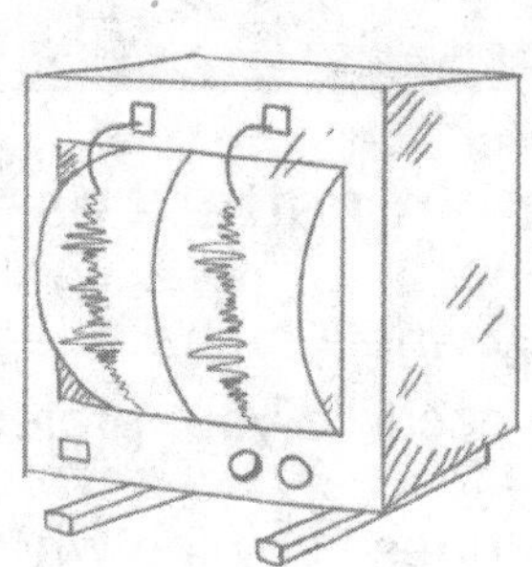

Planning after Lesson 3

Apply what you learned about preparing for earthquakes to continue your project planning.

What design features will you use in your models to help it withstand earthquake forces?

Research the Problem

 Read the Investigator article *Designing Strong Buildings*.

Research building designs by going online to teacher-approved websites, or by finding books on strong building designs at your local library.

Source	Information to Use in My Project

Sketch Your Model

Draw your ideas in the space below. Select two models to build and test.

STEM Module Project
Engineering Challenge

Design an Earthquake-Resistant Building

Look back at the planning you did after each lesson. Use that information to complete your final module project. As part of the design criteria, your models must remain standing after being placed on a table and shaken for 15 seconds. The constraint is that your model must measure between 15–30 cm (6–12 inches).

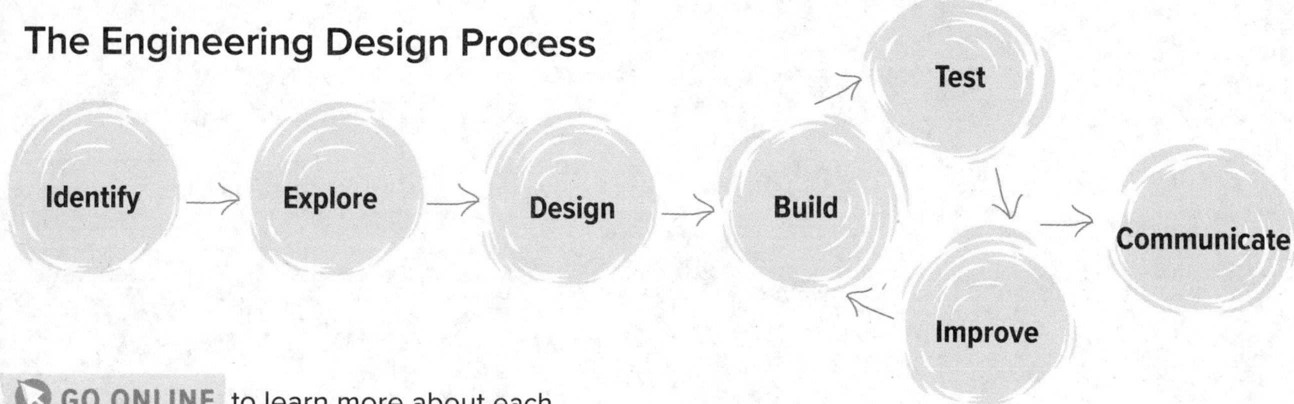

GO ONLINE to learn more about each step of the *Design Process*.

Build Your Model

1. Determine the problem you are trying to solve with your models.
2. Determine the criteria for your models, and list the materials you will use to build your models.
3. Use your project planning to build your models.
4. Record the steps of your procedure to carry out a fair test of your models.
5. Use the results of your test to compare your two models. Then select the design that best meets the criteria and constraints of the project.

Materials

Procedure:

Test Your Model

Record your observations and results. Use a data table or separate sheet of paper if needed. Select the design that best meets the criteria and present it to your class.

You are using the Engineering Design Process!

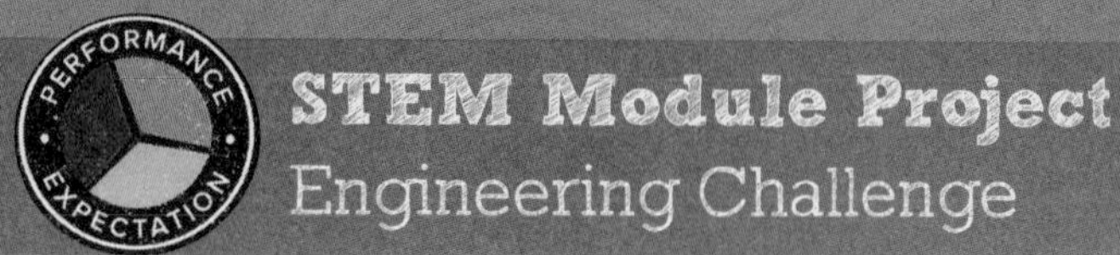

Communicate Your Results

Share the plan for your models and your results with another group. Compare how well each of your models was able to meet the criteria of withstanding the force of an earthquake. Discuss how well your models met the criteria and constraints, and identify ways you can improve your models. Communicate your findings below.

MODULE WRAP-UP

REVISIT THE PHENOMENON

Using what you have learned in this module, explain why this building collapsed, but the others did not.

How has your thinking changed? Explain.

Science Glossary

A

acceleration a change in velocity over time

adaptation a trait that helps a living thing survive in its environment

alternative energy source a source of energy other than the burning of a fossil fuel

amplitude a measure that relates to the amount of energy of a wave

B

binary code a system that represents letters, digits, or other characters using 0's and 1's

biofuel type of fuel made from biomass, or living or formerly living material

bracing diagonal pieces connecting beams and columns

brain organ in the nervous system that interprets messages received from and sends messages to other body organs

C

central nervous system part of the nervous system made up of the brain and spinal cord

chemical energy stored energy that is released when links between particles are broken or created

circuit a path through which electric current can flow

coding the process of writing a computer program in a language that can be used by a computer

collision when two or more objects crash into each other with a force

concave lens a lens that is thinner in the middle that always makes object look smaller

conduction the transfer of energy between two objects that are touching

conductor a material through which electricity flows easily

conservation the act of saving, protecting, or using resources wisely

conservation of energy a law that states that in a closed system, energy cannot be created or destroyed but can be transformed from one type into another

constraint something that limits or restricts someone or something

continent a large landmass

convection the transfer of energy in moving gases or liquid, such as warm air rising above a heater

convex lens a lens that is thicker in the middle that always makes object look larger

criteria standards on which a judgment or decision may be based

D

deposition the dropping off of eroded soil and bits of rock

design process a series of steps that engineers follow to come up with a solution to a problem

E

earthquake a sudden shaking of the rock that makes up Earth's crust

echolocation the process of finding an object by using reflected sound

electric current a flow of electricity through a conductor

energy the ability to do work

energy transfer the movement of energy from one object to another

erosion the movement of weathered material from one place to another.

external structures structures that are part of the outside of an organism's body

F

fault a break or crack in the rocks of Earth's crust where movement can take place

force a push or pull

fossil any remains or imprints of living things from the past

fossil fuel a source of energy made from the remains of ancient, once-living things

friction a force between surfaces that slows objects or stops them from moving

G

geothermal energy energy obtained from Earth's interior

H

heat the movement of energy from a warmer object to a cooler object

hydroelectricity electricity produced by waterpower

I

image a picture of the light source that light rays make in bouncing off a polished, shiny surface

inertia the tendency of an object in motion to stay in motion or of an object at rest to stay at rest

insulator a material that slows or stops the flow of energy, such as electricity or sound

internal structures structures that are found inside of an organism's body

L

landform a physical feature on Earth's surface

lateral force a force that comes from the sides

latitude the location north or south of the equator

longitude the location east or west from the Prime Meridian

longitudinal wave a wave vibrating in the same direction that the energy moves

M

magnitude the amount of energy released by an earthquake

medium a substance through which waves travel

motion a change in an object's position

N

natural resource something that is found in nature and is valuable to humans

nervous system the set of organs that use information from the senses to control all body systems

nonrenewable resource a natural material or source of energy that is useful to people and cannot be replaced easily

nuclear energy stored energy that is released when links between particles in the center of a particle of material are broken

O

opaque completely blocking light from passing through

P

peripheral nerve a nerve that is not part of the central nervous system and receives sensory information from cells in the body

plates large pieces that make up Earth's crust

pollution any harmful substance that affects Earth's land, air, or water

prototype an original or first model of something from which other forms are copied or developed

R

radiation energy that comes from a source in the form of waves or particles

reflection the bouncing of light waves off a surface

refraction the bending of light as it passes from one transparent material into another

renewable resource a useful material that is replaced quickly in nature

resistor an object that resists the flow of energy in an electrical circuit

response a reaction to a stimulus

S

sediment the particles of soil or rock that have been eroded and deposited

sedimentary rock a rock that forms when small bits of materials are pressed together in layers

seismic wave a vibration caused by an earthquake

seismograph an instrument used to detect and record earthquakes

sensory organ organs such as the skin, eyes, ears, nose, and tongue that gather information from outside the body

shear wall stiff wall made of braced panels

solar cell a device that uses light from the sun to produce electricity

solar power power obtained from solar energy to generate electricity using solar cells

sound wave a wave that transfers energy through material and spreads outward in all directions from a vibration

speed how fast an object's position changes over time at any given moment

spinal cord a thick bundle of nerves inside the spine

stimulus something in the environment that causes an action

structural adaptation an inherited change to physical features that helps an organism survive and reproduce

T

thermal energy the internal energy of an object due to the kinetic energy of its particles

topographic map a map that shows the elevation of an area of Earth's surface using contour lines

translucent letting only some light through, so objects on the other side appear blurry

transparent letting all the light through, so objects on the other side can be seen clearly

transpiration the release of water vapor, mainly through the small openings on the underside of leaves, that drives the movement of material throughout a plant

transverse wave a wave vibrating perpendicularly to the direction that the energy moves

tropism a plant's response to water, gravity, light, and touch

V

vegetation all the plants that cover a particular area

velocity the speed and direction of an object

vibration a back-and-forth motion

volcano an opening in Earth's surface where melted rock or gases are forced out

W

wavelength the distance from the top of one wave to the top of the next

weathering slow process that breaks materials into smaller pieces

Index

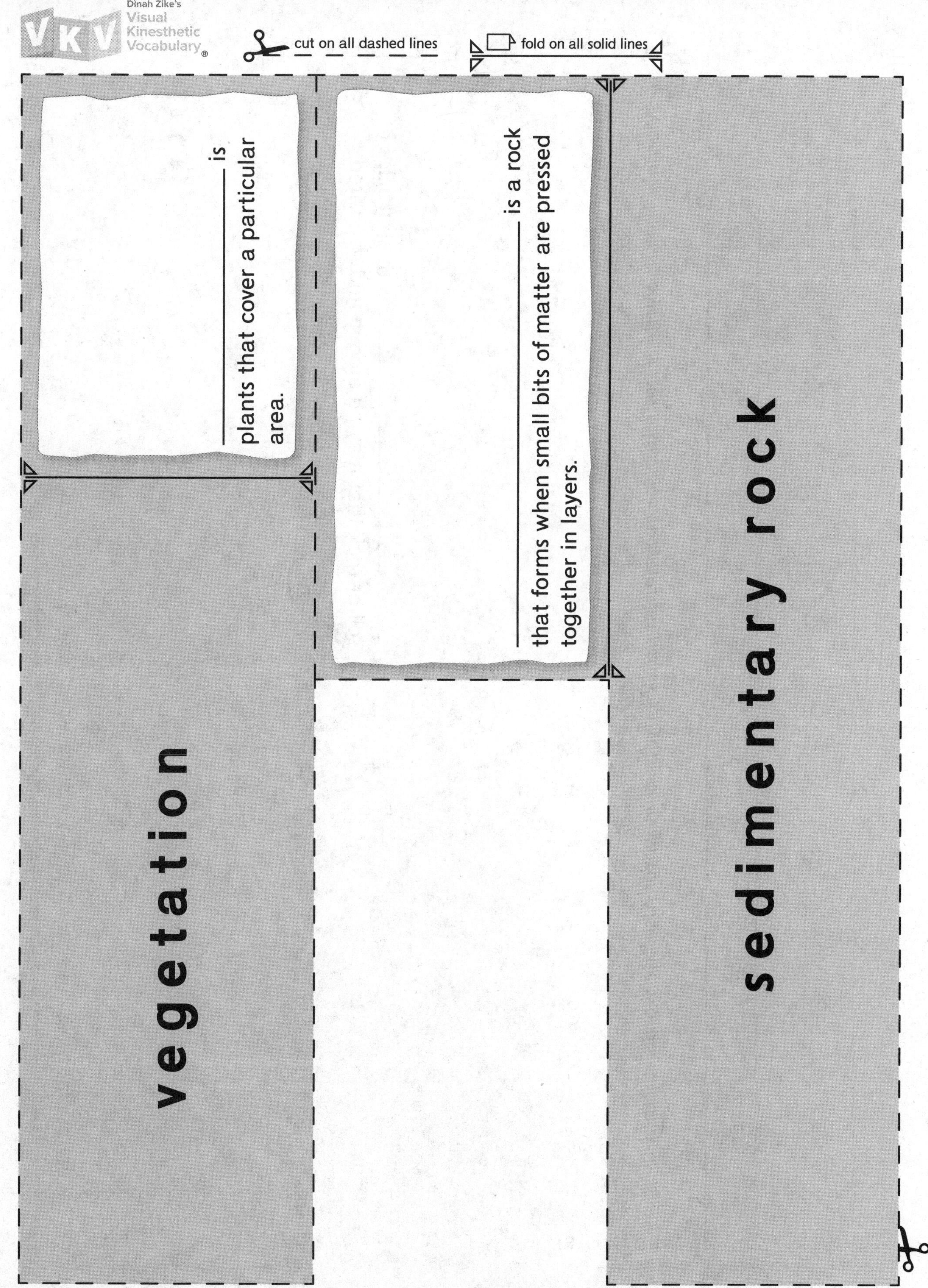

Dinah Zike's
Visual Kinesthetic Vocabulary®
VKV
cut on all dashed lines
fold on all solid lines
______ is plants that cover a particular area.
______ is a rock that forms when small bits of matter are pressed together in layers.
vegetation
sedimentary rock

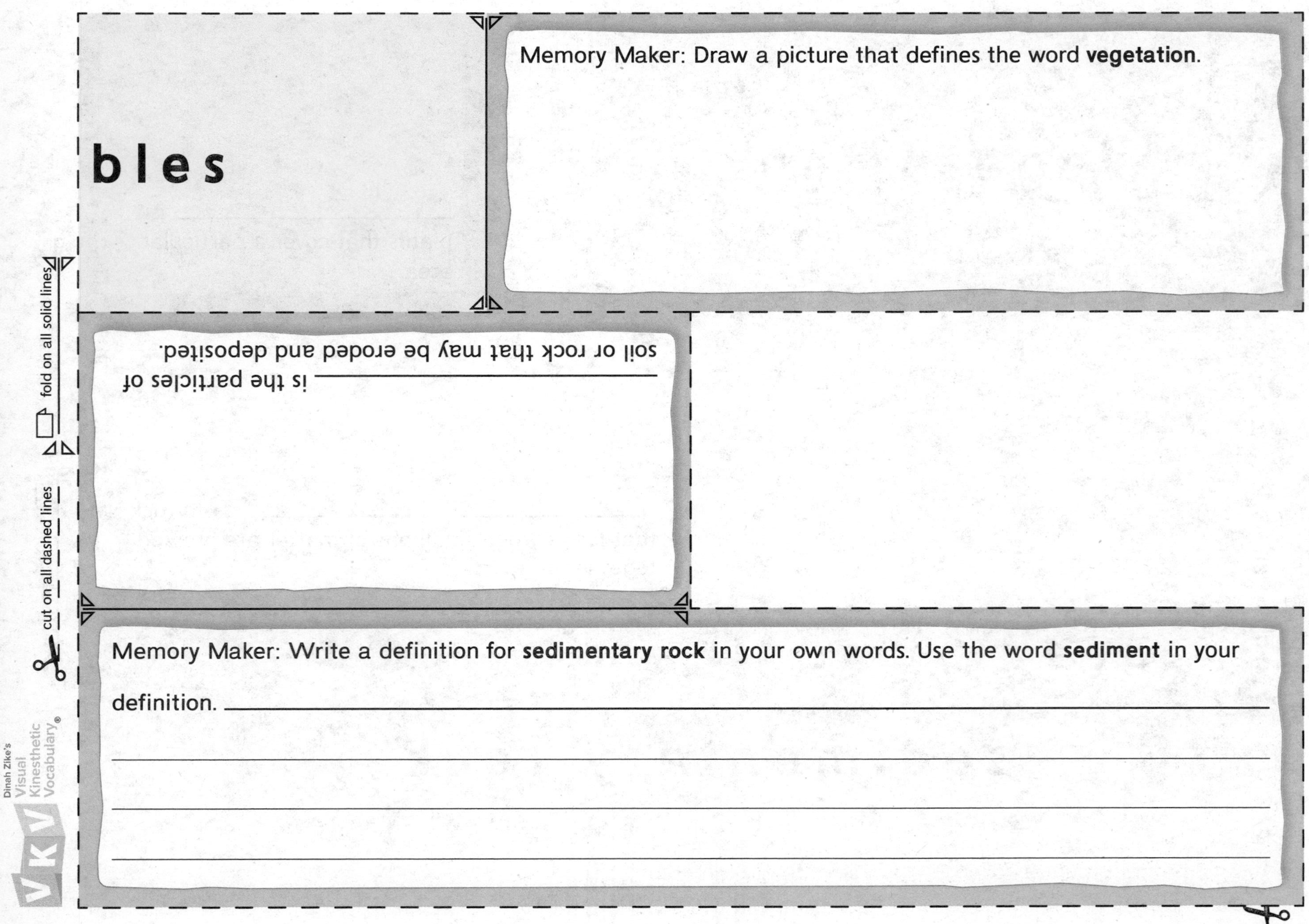

Dinah Zike's Visual Kinesthetic Vocabulary®

cut on all dashed lines

fold on all solid lines

Dinah Zike's Visual Kinesthetic Vocabulary®

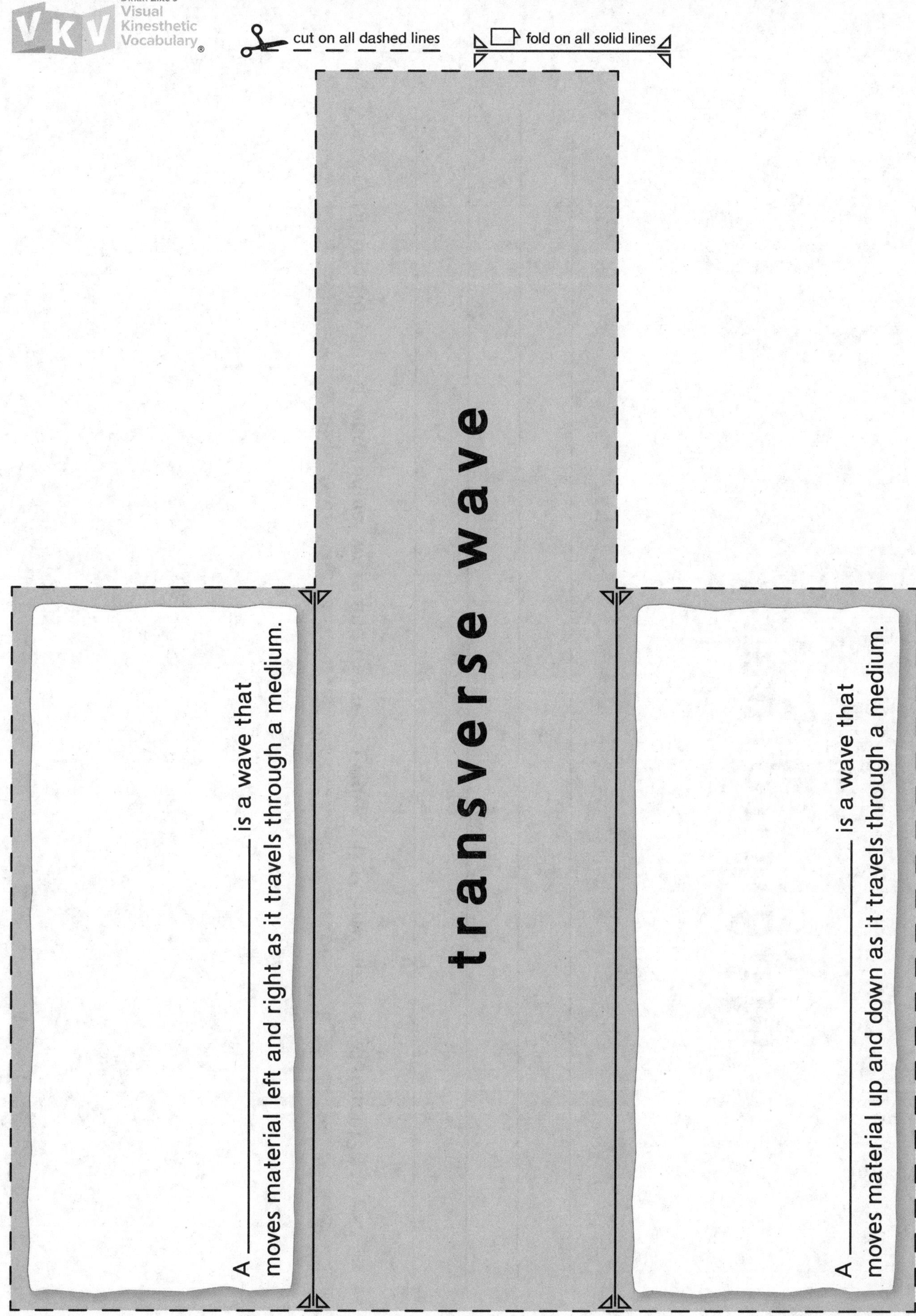

cut on all dashed lines

fold on all solid lines

Memory Maker: How are a **longitudinal wave** and **transverse wave** alike? How are they different?

longitudinal